The Very Best Business Handbook You'll Ever Own

(unless you use it as a bookend)

Mark Jarvis

ENDORSEMENTS

I wish this book had been there when I started my business! By far, this is the only book you need - it covers everything essential for achieving long-lasting success in both new and well-established businesses!

Olga Geidane,
Author and keynote speaker
on self-leadership and relationships.

Mark Jarvis's book is a masterclass in practical business wisdom, combining decades of real-world experience with actionable advice for entrepreneurs at all stages of their business journey.

Jamie McAnsh
Inspirational Keynote Speaker & TEDx Presenter,
Head of Inclusion for Champions (UK) Plc

Mark is a professional of the highest order, always adding value to conversations and being a go to person. His ability to understand issues and concerns of those around him is impactful and his support of clients is second to none.

Having selected this book read it on purpose, implement from its content and follow the process the chapters lead you through. There are some quick wins, some will take a little longer however providing it not used as a book end, you will with its content create the outcomes you desire.

Phillip Burton
Master Coach, Consultant and Trainer

Whether you're an aspiring entrepreneur or an established business leader, this handbook is your guide to achieving sustainable success. Keep it on your desk for when you need a quick boost of inspiration or a simple solution to a business problem. It's not just a book—it's your new business partner.

Claire Boscq
No 1 Woman Customer Experience Global Gurus
Keynote Speaker and The BizShui Creator

The Very Best Business Handbook You'll Ever Own

(unless you use it as a bookend)

Mark Jarvis

Publications

COPYRIGHT

Copyright ©Mark Jarvis August 2024.

Published: August 2024 Ladey Adey Publications, Ancaster, Lincolnshire UK.

Mark Jarvis has asserted his right to be identified as the author of this Work in accordance with the Copyright, Designs and Patents Act 1988.

ISBN: 978-1-913579-72-2 (Paperback).

ISBN: 978-1-913579-73-9 (E-Publication).

All rights reserved. No part of this publication may be reproduced, stored in a retrieval system, or transmitted in any form or by any means - for example, electronic, photocopy, recording - without the prior written permission of the publisher. The only exception is brief quotations in printed reviews.

British Library Cataloguing-in-Publication Data.
A catalogue record for this book is available from The British Library.

Cover Design by Abbirose Adey, of Ladey Adey Publications.

Neither the author nor the publisher can be held responsible for any loss, claim or damage arising out of the use, or misuse of the suggestions made, the failure to take business, financial or legal advice or for any material on third party websites.

The author and publisher has made every effort to ensure the external websites included in this book are correct and up to date at the time of going to press. The author and publisher are not responsible for the content, quality or continuing accessibility of the sites.

While direct reproductions of this book are restricted, please feel free to use the content as you wish. Much of the content is wisdom learned over time and what I recall learning from others. However, an acknowledgement of the book would be appreciated if the content is used.

If you have enjoyed this book please give a review on Amazon® for Mark.

Contents

Chapter Blurbs vii
Foreword xvii
Introduction xxi
How To Achieve The Second Goal Of Every Business Owner 1
How To Avoid The Catch When Finding Your Purpose 11
How To Get Recruitment Right First Time - Part 1 19
How To Get Recruitment Right First Time - Part 2 25
How To Leverage AI In Business 35
How To Avoid Random Acts of Delegation 45
Why Start-ups Sometimes Fail 57
Getting The Business Basics Right 8 Tips For Success 61
Why Creative Distraction Is Holding You Back 65
The Secret to Cultural Success in Business 71
What We Can Learn From Not-For-Profit Organisations 77
How To Unlock The Power Of Focus 85
The Key To Organisational Health 93
The Five Things To Do When Creating A Team Skills Development Plan ... 99
Make it Better Before Trying to Make it Bigger 103
Be, Do, Have - What Does it Mean? 107
Why Do Drama When Drama-free Is A Choice? 109
Why People Leave People 111
What Are The Four Things On The Mind Of Every Business Owner? ... 115
Is Today Your Last Groundhog Day? 117
How To Solve The Problem Of The Entrepreneurs Second See-Saw 121
What's Your Inner Geek?* 125
What Are Big Goals And What Are Ordinary Goals? 129
What Trust Should Be 131
Possibilities And Probabilities 133
The Reality Of Referrals In Business 135
Dunbar's Number And Why You Should Care 143
Why Defining Your Target Market Shouldn't Be So Hard 147
Why Aren't You More Profitable In Your Network? 149
Why Are My Clients Not Held Accountable? 153
Plan For Increased Productivity Through Professional Networking 155
How Do You Know If Those In Your Network Are The Right People? ... 159
Igniting Conversations 161
What Does Making Changes In Business Really Mean? 163
Which Came First, Sales Pipeline Or The Relationship Pipeline? 167

What Is Customer Service Really?	171
What Makes A Great Footballer?	173
What Will You Let Go Of First?	175
Ten Ways To Say Thank You	177
Five Key Ways To Build Customer Relationships	181
It's Not The Ingredients, It's What You Do With Them	185
How To Keep Your Battery Charged	187
The Ultimate Guide, Or How To Build A Better Business	191
Know, Like, Trust - What Does It Really Mean?	193
The 60:20:20 Rule (From The Jarvis Principles)	197
The Top Seven Barriers To Consistent Quality Referrals	203
The Difference Between Word Of Mouth And Referral Marketing	205
Which Question I Am Asked Most Often	209
Meaningful Goals	213
The Perpetual Motion Business	215
Why Running A Business Should Be Like Driving A Car	217
What's The Difference Between A Teacher, A Coach, And A Mentor?	219
What Does Packard's Law Teach Us About Business Growth?	223
Time Limited Turnover - The Eternal Business Challenge	225
Five Top Tips For Managing A Growing Team	229
Are You Working In Transaction World Or Relationship World?	235
How Much Does It Cost To Hire A Business Coach?	237
About the Author	**245**
Endorsements	**247**
Acknowledgements	**251**
References	**253**
Index	**257**
Your Notes	**261**

Here's your key to this handbook; handy icons for you to scroll through on the edge of each page to find the topics ideas you're looking fo .
You will also see some chapters cover multiple topics, the topmost icon being the primary topic.

⊛	Time Saving and Time Management
⛰	Profitabilit , Cash Flow, Making and Saving Money
⊚	Teams, Leadership, Organisational Culture and Vision
⬣	Marketing, Sale and Lead Generation
≈	General Experiences, Ideas and Insight Learned across 30+ years in business

Chapter Blurbs
A Summary Of The Topics Covered

As this book is a handbook, I felt it would be useful to let you have a brief synopsis of each chapter, a 'blurb' for each if you will. Each synopsis will give you an impression of the content and help you dive into your chosen topic.

 How To Achieve The Second Goal Of Every Business Owner (page 1)

The first goal everyone wants is: to work less hours for more money, the second most common goal for business owners and leaders, how do I get my business to run without me? Or, how do I take a step back?

 How To Avoid The Catch When Finding Your Purpose (page 11)

To really embrace a life of purpose, whether it's in the marketplace or the not-for-profit world, and to really stand out in an increasingly competitive world, you must accept that you need to move away from being an end and become a means to an end that is not you.

 How To Get Recruitment Right First Time - Part 1 (page 19)

As you grow and scale your business, getting recruitment right can be a challenge. It's getting increasingly difficult t attract quality candidates without offering budget-busting salaries and benefits pac ages. What's the answer?

How To Get Recruitment Right First Time - Part 2 (page 25)

Growing your business with the right people can be a challenge, especially for early-stage and high-growth businesses. In this chapter, I'm going to explore some of the key points to think more closely about to help you get recruitment right first time

 How To Leverage AI In Business (page 35)

There are many different ways to use AI, my favourite is to use it while I'm brainstorming a project or researching a topic - this chapter for example.

 How To Avoid Random Acts Of Delegation (page 45)

The topic of delegation makes most people groan, its something we all know we need to do and get better at, yet most people don't really know what it means beyond giving tasks to others. Delegation, when done right, is a leadership development strategy.

 Why Start-Ups Sometimes Fail (page 57)

The first year of every start-up is, or should be, focussed on 'problem market fit', which means you ask the question does your market care about the problem you're solving?

 Getting The Business Basics Right - 8 Tips For Success (page 61)

Remember, growing a business takes time, patience, commitment and persistence. Don't be afraid to experiment with different strategies, ask for help, and be willing to adapt and pivot as needed to achieve your goals.

 Why Creative Distraction Is Holding You Back (page 65)

Whenever you are tempted to opt for immediate over ultimate, or want now over value most, or opt for optional over what's essential, you are choosing to change your priorities from what's important to what you perceive is urgent.

The Secret To Cultural Success In Business (page 71)
When your mission is clear and you live it every day, you are hiring the right people because you can, not because you must, and you have a winning culture, you have the seeds of success.

 What Can We Learn From Not-For-Profit Organisations? (page 77)
Not-for-profit, charities and social enterprises have always known purpose drives their organisation. As business owners, this is a very profitable lesson to learn

 How To Unlock The Power Of Focus (page 85)
By working to your strengths, your organisation will become more intelligent, more productive, and more profitable

 The Key To Organisational Health (page 93)
The success of your organisation is not based on your intelligence or the tactical decisions you make, but it's based on your character and your ability to build a healthy organisation through day-to-day and simple disciplines.

 The Five Most Important Things to Do When Creating a Team Skills Development Plan (page 99)
A well-designed plan not only enhances individual growth but also fosters a culture of collaboration and innovation within the team. In this chapter, we will explore the five most important things to consider when creating a team skills development plan.

 Make It Better Before Trying To Make It Bigger (page 103)
If you are going to make anything better, you have to decide what better looks like and what it means. You have to seek clarification before evaluation

 Be, Do, Have - What Does It Mean? (page 107)
Put as simply as possible, this concept is all about BEING the person you want to be and DOING the right things in order to HAVE the life and experiences you want.

Why Do Drama When Drama-Free Is A Choice? (page 109)
Is it true, is it kind, is it helpful. What have you heard, seen or listened to today where these 3 points are true?

Why People Leave People (page 111)
Learning how to create an environment of clear, inclusive and collaborative communication is a key step in increasing long term loyalty in your team, and it starts with you.

 What are The Four Things On The Mind Of Every Business Owner (page 115)
Saving time, making more money, and building a stronger culture in business are three of the most important things for business owners. What's the fourth you may ask? Simply how? How will you get there?.

 Is Today Your Last Groundhog Day (page 117)
Scaling a business requires that people change because when people change, those people can change things - not the other way around.

 How To Solve The Problem Of The Entrepreneurs Second See-Saw (page 121)
The second see-saw; "I need to take on someone, but I can't afford to until I get more business, but I can't get more business until I employ someone".

What's Your Inner Geek?* (page 125)
We all know the only constant in life is change. Unless you are investing in positive change, negative change is inevitable.

What Are Big Goals And What Are Ordinary Goals? (page 129)
All goals are good, but are they big goals? Are they simply ordinary goals, not because they are any less valuable, but because once achieved, you have to go on and set another goal, and another?

What Trust Should Be (page 131)
Trust is about having faith in the integrity of others. Integrity is not about who we are, what we've done, our achievements or accolades, but what we are.

Possibilities And Probabilities (page 133)
Don't let negative possibilities hold you back; decide to change by focusing on one positive possibility today and then seek support to make that possibility a reality.

The Reality Of Referrals In Business Today (page 135)
How you can open up your own five Levels of Referral for more profitable busines

Dunbar's Number And Why You Should Care (page 143)
Relationships not connections drive our world, whether in business or personally. Building a strong sustainable business means building your relationships and growing your network.

Why Defining Your Target Market Shouldn't Be So Hard (page 147)
When doing business by relationship, you CAN still do business in any industry, you will just be doing business with the people who share your values and beliefs.

Why Aren't You More Profitable In Your Network (page 149)
Profitability is a long-term strategy that can win your company massive amounts of business by building strong relationships and credibility in your network.

Why Are My Clients Not Held Accountable? (page 153)
We are hard-wired to resist change. Yet change is the one thing we seek when thinking about growth. You want to grow but are you willing enough to change?

How To Plan For Increased Productivity Through Professional Networking (page 155)

This chapter is about the process of assessing and developing your professional network so you are able to effectively develop yourself and your business

 How Do You Know If Those In Your Network Are The Right People? (page 159)

This chapter is about the process of assessing and developing your professional network based around working with the right people.

≈ **Igniting Conversations (page 161)**

When in conversation, are you listening to react or listening to respond. Even though our passion can be very engaging, make sure it's not at the expense of listening.

≈ **What Does Making Changes In Business Really Mean (page 163)**

Change is about creating a different outcome, not about creating a list of things to change. The results you create for your business are not just different, they are bette .

 Which Came First, The Sales Pipeline Or The Relationship Pipeline (page 167)

For every eight hours I invest in my Relationship Pipeline, I have the opportunity for infinite referrals. Whereas for every 84 hours I invest in my Sales Pipeline, I have the opportunity for one sale.

 What Is Customer Service Really? (page 171)

Why do we focus so much of our money, time and energy on customer service? The simple answer is because customer service is, in reality, reputation management.

≈ **What Makes A Great Footballer (page 173)**

The game of football is often called 'The Beautiful Game' and perhaps the beauty is in playing the game...and not winning the game.

What Will You Let Go Of First? (page 175)
When it comes time to sell your business, what will you let go of first?

Ten Ways To Say 'Thank You' (page 177)
Research shows that customers spend more, employees accomplish more, and suppliers are more likely to raise their game, if they're thanked regularly.

Five Ways To Build Customer Relationships (page 181)
If our home is all about location, location, location, then small business is all about relationships, relationships, relationships. Find them, nurture them, and watch your sales soar.

It's Not The Ingredients, It's What You Do With Them (page 185)
Success comes from the way ingredients are combined, crafted and shaped over time. I make an awesome cake and it's not because I have the best ingredients, it's because I know how to combine them.

How To Keep Your Battery Charged (page 187)
What happens if your battery is not fully charged each day? The amount of time and energy you have to invest in the activities in your day is decreased.

The Ultimate Guide, Or How To Build A Better Business (page 191)
Six questions to ask yourself to build a better, stronger and smarter business and leave it in a better place than when you started.

Know, Like, Trust - What Does It Really Mean? (page 193)
Know, Like and Trust forms the basis of any relationship, whether business or personal. What if we used this principle to build better business, not just more business?

The 60:20:20 Rule (From The Jarvis Principles) (page 197)

To guarantee growth, I believe people should be working 60% of their time in their business, 20% of their time on their business, and 20% of their time on themselves.

 The Top Seven Barriers To Consistent Quality Referrals (page 203)

What prevents referrals is superficially simple - not asking, asking too early or not following up. This is about what stops consistent quality, which is somewhat different

 The Difference Between Word Of Mouth And Referral Marketing (page 205)

Referral marketing is measurable and repeatable. It can be controlled, focused and targeted. Word- of-mouth is more about reaction and spontaneity.

 Which Question I Am Asked Most Often (page 209)

Grow your business by surrounding yourself with people who have already achieved what you want to achieve, and learn from them.

 Meaningful Goals (page 213)

Reviewing your numbe rs this year and simply adding a few zero's to next year's goals won't cut it if you are truly committed to scaling your business.

 The Perpetual Motion Business (page 215)

Start with disciplined people, give them the responsibility to succeed and the knowledge to implement and we can all build an efficient busines

 Why Running A Business Should Be Like Driving A Car (page 217)

Driving a car requires all sorts of skills and learning and I believe the principles of running a business and driving a car are very similar, and here's why.

What's The Difference Between A Teacher, A Mentor And A Coach? (page 219)

Rarely does anyone find success without having one or two people around them to help, support and guide them, and this is as true in business as it is personally.

 What Does Packard's Law Teach Us About Business Growth? (page 223)

Growing a productive team is much more than just recruiting based on demand. To grow a productive team requires starting with the right people.

 Time Limited Turnover - The Eternal Business Challenge. (page 225)

Time limited turnover is a phenomenon familiar to all of us who have ever started a business, grown a business or worked in a business.

 Five Top Tips For Managing A Growing Team. (page 229)

A growing team can bring new and exciting opportunities for a business. From experience to fresh ideas, new team members can drive a business forward and inject energy into an established team.

 Are You Working In Transaction World Or Relationship World? (page 235)

In transaction world, our currency is money. In relationship world our currency is trust. Trust is the only currency which matters, here's why.

 How Much Does It Cost To Hire A Business Coach? (page 237)

When thinking about getting help, most people have three burning questions - I have done ok so far, why would I need any help? How much will it cost? How long will it take?

Foreword

I have been invited to contribute a foreword to this book and my goal is to give you some insights about the author. I have known Mark for over 20 years and hope to encourage you to buy, read and use the wisdom from this book. I was thrilled to see he is sharing his knowledge in a book and the main attraction for me, not surprisingly as my own business works on the same principle, is the simple approach to his topic.

What he has going for him:

Mark has a lot going for him and a lot of what he has going for him and which has been shared in this book is going to help you as a business owner!

- He has age and experience on his side! Someone once said age and experience will always win over youth and enthusiasm but Mark is old enough to know what he is talking about but has the enthusiasm of youth.
- He is extremely bright and remains humble and open to other's ideas and messages. He is a great listener.
- He is thoughtful in the real sense of the word. I often wonder if Auguste Rodin might have met Mark in another life when he created his great sculpture, *The Thinker*!
- He is generous. He charges fees for a lot of the information in this book, now you can access that

- for the price of the book and it will feel like he is supporting you in person.
- He and I share one inarguable truth. There is a tendency in the knowledge industry for experts to over complicate stuff so they can charge a lot to unravel the complexities and the reality is it was simple in the first place

Mark has some faults too!

- He is tenacious and is the king of follow up. This habit of doing what he says he is going to do and holding himself and others to account and upholding high standards is annoying to some people!
- He is able to take big topics and distil them into a tasty potion - some people will want more information but heed this warning - just because you have a lot doesn't mean to say you have what you need.
- He knows loads more stuff, but he has edited this book to within an inch of its life to help your learning. It is often harder to say less than more but he has done just this and some of you may want more. That is OK, I am sure he could be encouraged to write a sequel! Each section could almost be a book in its own right!

How to read the book

This is up to you and how you learn. The temptation will be to just dive into the topic title which interests you the most and dip in and out when needed. How you approach this learning will depend on what outcomes you are looking for. So ask yourself, "What am I looking to get from this book?"

In a world where knowledge and resources are plentiful and you can get what you need, when you need it at your fingertips quickly, why bother reading a whole book all the way through and even read it again a second time? We have been seduced away from a solid, consistent approach to learning. So we can end up knowing a little about a lot or making judgements based on false assumptions.

Mark knows a lot about a lot and he has blessed the pages of this book with high value which, again, is not always found in today's world.

For what it is worth, my suggestion is to read all the way through first. Even if you do it quickly at first. Then make a note of what you are really trying to achieve and the areas of the book which are most relevant to your current position. This way you can prioritise what needs to be considered and approached in the right order. Remember you aren't just mulling over some of these ideas to never implement them. If you have picked up this book you are ready to seriously apply some learning which works so even though Mark always doesn't take himself too seriously, take the content very seriously as the impact it will make on your life is likely to be bigger than you can ever imagine.

Sarah Owen
Founder of DISCsimple
Host of the long running weekly show - DISClive
New York Best-selling Author

Mark Jarvis

Introduction

To say I am the author of this book is perhaps rather a misnomer. I am rather, your guide through all the information I have collected since the early 1990s about what it takes to start, scale and sell the businesses I've founded. Much of it I learned from others but perhaps much more of it I learned the hard way though my own mistakes and frustrations.

My aim is simple; to give you what I've learned in easy to follow and accessible, bite-sized chunks so that you can move forward with your business without making all the mistakes I did.

The three behaviours which make me mad:

1. Too many people trying to make starting, scaling and selling a business complicated so they can justify over-inflated fees and a holier-than-thou attitude. Business is simple (not simplistic), it's just not easy if you don't know how.
2. The belief that more and more knowledge will automatically bring the revelation you hope for. Trust me it won't. I can't tell you how much time I've wasted on, courses and workshops and endlessly chasing the next best answer when the solution lies in probably my most favourite saying ever: "Only do what only you can do".
3. Trying to short-cut human behaviour, whether you're building and leading your team or through

the use of technology in your marketing, sales and customer service. Until we have a computer chip embedded in our brain, we still work by building relationships and communities.

Rant over, I'll climb down from my enormously high soapbox... Seriously though, it's a huge frustration for me that so many business owners, perhaps just like you, feel more and more overwhelmed, more and more of the time, when there's so much help available if only they become brave enough to ask. Oops, first step back on the soapbox!

Anyway, why is this book called *"The Very Best Business Handbook You'll Ever Own..."* I'm very aware that there are hundreds of business books out there, many of them written by amazingly accomplished authors, and far better written than I could ever hope to achieve. What I believe is missing, is the practical application of all those tips and ideas I've learned in business since the 1990s, and in a career journey starting way back in the late 1970s.

This then is all I've learned so far, from a practical point of view - never complicated (I hope), and never self-absorbed, so you can dip in and out and get simple ideas to support your own business journey. That's it really. I've indexed the topics with some little icons so you can thumb through and find what's relevant to you. See, it's a handbook...

I wish you every success in your journey.

Mark

There are further resources and downloads here www.mark-jarvis.co.uk and please do share your successes and questions.

Finally, I too, am still learning and regularly adding to this content, if you're interested in a digital quarterly update, drop me an email here: mark@mark-jarvis.co.uk

Let's Dive In ...

Mark Jarvis

How To Achieve The Second Goal Of Every Business Owner

The challenge we're going to talk about today is one all leaders face, but too many of them face it alone. I've been teaching, coaching and mentoring business owners and leaders for over two decades now and these same points come up time and time again. The first goal everyone wants is to work less hours for more money, and this is as much true for those in a role as it is for business owners. In fact, it's true for everyone. If you were offered more holidays for the same salary, would you take it, of course you would. If you could increase your profits without working harder, would you? Of course you would, if only you knew how.

Today's topic is all about the second most common goal for business owners and leaders. **How do I get my business to run without me, or how do I take a step back?** Today, I'm going to give you a way to do this.

Today we're going to talk about vision. Before you start thinking 'not that again', I'm going to show you a way to think about vision differentl , in a way that's more meaningful and useful.

Every leader understands the importance of vision but as your business begins to grow, so vision begins to leak, it dulls, and it gets lost in the complexity of organisational life. You believe you've covered it, perhaps in your monthly meetings but the reality is, we never talk about or share and project the vision enough. We assume people heard what we said, and we think people are sharing it too, but the bucket leaks as the vision is projected through the organisation.

WE'RE BUILDING VISION PROMOTERS

My career started in the hotel and hospitality industry and latterly I was part of the team that trained the staff in some of the biggest hotel chains in Europe. The single biggest impact on customer experience in this and every industry is the ability of the customer facing staff to promote the vision of the organisation. For most staff, they simply cannot because the vision had got lost before it even reached them - how on earth could they then promote the vision and deliver an exceptional experience to customers!

YOUR TEAM CARRY THEIR VERSION OF YOUR VISION

Remember the 'leaky bucket' analogy and the fact messages become diluted as they filter through the organisation. It's the same with vision. If you are not continually talking about, sharing and promoting the vision, your team will carry and promote their own version. **Scaling a successful organisation really is about how you work the vision into everything you and your team does. It becomes the very core of your purpose.**

FOUR LITTLE WORDS THAT CAN KILL VISION PROMOTION

"It's not my job". When it comes to vision promotion, it's easy to think it's the job of the business owner or leader when in fact it's everyone's job. Those four little words and the attitude behind them is one of the most common reasons you cannot take a step back or hand over responsibility in your business and achieve the second goal.

Everyone in your organisation should be carrying and promoting the vision.

Everyone represents your organisation in some way, whether it's how they talk about it outside of work, how they talk to each other, or how they talk to your customers and suppliers. Your job is helping them to understand the role they are already fulfilling, helping them to do a better job, and gain acknowledgement for their achievements.

Way back in my hotel industry days, one of our main training challenges was making sure the company's vision and brand values were filtering through the whole organisation so when a customer called to make a booking, their experience was consistent with what they actually experienced with the front-line staff, and right through their stay in the hotel. **Their perception matched their experience.**

Are your front-line and customer facing staff able to carry and promote the vision that you as the business owner or leader created. Is your whole team able to carry and promote the vision when they talk to each other and talk outside of work. Until they can, your business will never be able to grow and scale without you. It may tick along quite nicely while you take a holiday etc. but **truly letting go is impossible unless your team can carry and promote the vision into future generations of the organisation.**

HERE ARE TWO THINGS THAT GET IN THE WAY

Working with as many organisations as I have over the years, there are a few things that get in the way of empowering every level in your team to become a vision carrier and promoter.

The first reason: many organisations don't have a vision that is promotable. By this I mean it's not crystal clear at the top so there's no way it can ever by carried or promoted by your team. **"If it's misty at the top, it'll be foggy on the ground."** If the vision is even a little unclear for you as owner and leader, it's going to get even less clear for the second, third and fourth tier in the organisation. One of the ways this shows up in an organisation is in your

Net Promotor Score (Google it), because your customers' experiences are not matching up to their expectations.

The second thing which gets in the way is that sometimes as leaders, we confuse responsibility and role. As the business owner, leader or director, you understand that your role is to promote vision, but that's different to the responsibility every single person in the organisation has to carry it. If that responsibility is not communicated to me as an employee, then I'm not going to do it, not necessarily because I don't want to, but because I can't.

We all have those pivotal moments in our careers when we learned something which changed our world. One of those for me was back in 2005 when I attended a team meeting led by one of my team, Ben. Ben was an emerging leader to whom I had delegated responsibility and ownership of a project. Anyway, the meeting I attended was one of our regular monthly review and planning sessions so I wasn't expecting anything out of the usual, but what changed my life was seeing and hearing Ben carry, project and promote the vision to his team is such a way I began to think to myself, I could pack up and leave it all to you because you're doing a better job at promoting vision than I did. It was such a proud and thrilling moment and gave me the leverage to achieve that second goal - how to take a step back and the business (almost) runs itself.

I've found that many business owners, leaders or directors have never experienced the rush, the joy, the thrill of sitting in a meeting and watching another leader in the organisation promote an even more compelling vision than they've been able to.

If you are even going to be in a position to take a step back from your business and have it run by itself, not just in the short term, but for future generations, I believe you must work towards building your team with vision carriers and promoters.

Your aim should be to transition your people from 'benefiting from the vision' to 'participating in the vision'. Your employees benefit from the vision at its most basic level, because they have a job in a growing organisation but empowering them to participate in the vision requires additional focus and planning, (if you want some help, drop me a line).

We've all heard of word-of-mouth marketing, what it actually means in the context we are discussing today, is that your customers become vision carriers and promoters too! In marketing terminology this means creating raving fans. Every satisfied customer carries the vision you created when they talk about your products or services, whether it's a hotel experience, food or any other kind of product or service. We've all experienced this when we talk about a positive experience with our friends. We don't think of it as promoting a vision, it's just sharing experiences, but it's still part of what we are talking about today.

Our world is changing faster than ever with free access to information about anything, anytime we want it. This is giving our customers more control than ever, with more credibility than ever. It's one thing to sell a product or service and provide an exceptional customer experience. It's a completely different thing for that customer to then go on and promote your business to others.

LET'S TAKE THIS A STEP FURTHER

What's the one question every one of your prospects asks? Not out loud but this is the bottom line: **Does this business or organisation care about me now?** The degree to which you can get your customer to answer that question with a yes, is equal to the number of raving fans you are creating, which connects to the number of customers who carry the vision, and the number of customers who promote the vision. **Do you really care about your customers, do you care about your people** or do you just care about growing your business? Perhaps this is something worth taking to your marketing team and all the social media noise created when people just shout about what they're doing.

LET'S CIRCLE BACK TO TODAY'S QUESTION - HOW CAN I GET MY BUSINESS TO RUN WITHOUT ME?

We've talked about the clear link between word-of-mouth, creating raving fans and vision promotors in our customers. Now let's transfer this into our team. Creating raving fans in your team may sound a little strange, after all, it's expected that your staff will automatically rave about their employer. I think we all know this is not true in many cases. If it were, no one would ever resign!

One of the simplest ideas I implemented is to get everybody together in the morning and say *"today our goal and our mission is to let everyone know that we really care about each other and the people that we will interact with"*. What was the result? Fans and vision carriers who felt involved, energised and inspired. They talked with each other and others, inside and outside the organisation. These vision carriers then go on to become vision promoters which means you are creating a culture and vision in an organisation which doesn't rely on one person (you) to carry it.

The next thing I did was to capture and share stories, and systemise the process. We all know the power of stories, good marketeers and salespeople use them all the time.

My learning was that there is incredible power in stories when shared internally. Let's say you have team of 25, doesn't have to be 25 but in an organisation around this number, not everybody talks with everybody else every day. So capturing and sharing customer and staff stories in team meetings proved to be a game-changer in terms of **how the team knew we cared about each other and** our customers, which empowered them to own and carry the vision forward.

Include some time in your team meetings where you capture, share and record stories, not just file them away as testimonials or case studies.

Taking this a step further - ask yourself "What did I do today to promote the vision?"

The key word there is 'today'. It's easy for us to say you're working on something, or something great is happening soon, but there has to be something every day. It doesn't have to be huge; it can be just a small thing like a thank you card to a customer or catching a team member doing a great job. Of course there have been many times when I've looked at myself and said, I was so busy, I did nothing today to promote the vision. My advice to myself and to you is to make this one of the top priorities you do everyday because if somehow, you get so busy and forget the 'today' part, then you are not being the best leader you can possibly be, which means your goal of stepping back is not getting any closer.

When you and those who report to you do this with their teams too, and you do this on a daily basis, like anything, it begins to build habit and momentum. Your mind is open to more ideas, and you're collecting more stories, and your meetings take a more inspirational tone rather than an informational tone.

Here are three things you can do to start moving towards a position where your business runs without you.

Start where you are: the first suggestion I can give you is to do what I call it 'vision inventory'. You can do this by simply asking your team, "What do you think is the vision of our organisation and why are we here?" You are probably going to hear some things that encourage you and you're going to hear some things that discourage you, but you need to find out where you are starting from. Do a vision inventory and don't assume people understand why they are here.

Use what you have: I think sometimes in the business world we think if we had more money we could do more things. Many times more money creates less thinking because you have a lot more resources. In terms of word of mouth, there are things you can do that don't cost you anything. I believe social media has a place, but it can be overinflated, and most of it is free and an ideal place to carry and promote the vision internally and externally.

Do what you can: this goes back to, 'What did you do today to promote the vision?' It's not about conquering the world, but you can do one thing every day to promote vision through others who can carry it and promote it themselves.

What I hope I've been able to show you today is that to let go, you have to hand over responsibility to others. Not just responsibility for tasks and activities but to hand over responsibility for carrying and promoting the vision to others throughout your organisation and on through your customers to your prospects. **Now you're building an organisation that has a future without you and into future generations.**

To refuse to do so is simply going to ensure that when you leave your department, division or organisation, the vision is going to leave with you. If your goal is for everybody to think back on the good old days when you were at the helm, then keeping responsibility for vision to yourself is an excellent way to ensure that outcome because the vision left with you. If you want to build a multi-generational organisation, something that's not simply going to outlive you, but maybe even be better after you, you've got to raise up vision promotors and create vision carriers at every level in the organisation. That's your role.

See also
How To Avoid Random Acts Of Delegation - A Leadership Strategy (p45)
What We Can Learn From Not-For-Profit Organisations (p77)
The Key To Organisational Health (p93)
The Five Most Important Things To Do When Creating A Team Skills Development Plan (p99)
Which Came First, The Sales Pipeline Or The Relationship Pipeline (p167)

How To Assess The Value Of Your Goals

There are key times in the year when we naturally review our goals so I thought I would share with you three questions which I hope will help you assess the value of the goals you are thinking about.

Rather than waffl on about the importance of setting goals and having a plan, I've found these three questions really help me stay on track to set and achieve meaningful goals in both life and business.

Here they are:

1. Is the value of the goal worth the sacrifice required to achieve it?
2. Is the reward in the journey worth your time?
3. Do you have the discipline required to keep going even through set-backs?

If you can't answer yes to those three questions, then seriously ask yourself whether you are setting the right goals, or whether you need a different approach

Need help setting meaningful goals, contact me at mark@mark-jarvis.co.uk

How To Avoid The Catch When Finding Your Purpose

When I first started thinking about this topic, I thought about finding a different title because I've written about purpose already. You could look at this article as Part 2, though I will explore the full scope of the topic here too.

FINDING YOUR PURPOSE CAN BE UNEXPECTEDLY COMPLEX

As we're about to discover, purpose has a catch. Whereas everyone is inspired find their purpose, embrace purpose and bring purpose into your organisation and to your market, there's a catch. There's an obstacle that can get in the way, and I think one of the reasons more leaders aren't more successful in embracing the idea of purpose, whether it's in the for-profit or not-for-profit world, is they're not aware of the catch and they unknowingly bump up against it.

It could be argued that early on in the evolution of a business, or early on in your career, purpose is not all that important simply because you are focussed on staying afloat, growing your business or planning your career path. So when you are getting started, purpose can be seen as a 'nice to have' one day soon. Meanwhile, you need to sell your stuff, you've got to account for stuff, manage stuff, read stuff, lead your team and get paid. Purpose often hovers out there somewhere as something you'll look at in the future, but eventually you'll bump into the question, 'Why am I doing this?' and, 'What is this leading to?' Eventually purpose becomes a big deal and the sooner you can address this vital topic, the sooner the path to your future will become clear.

PURPOSE IS ALWAYS ASSOCIATED WITH VISION

Whether it's a product, vision for a product or service, something new or making something better, there's always a connection between vision and purpose. Purpose provides the momentum to move you towards your vision and through life's barriers that would otherwise slow you or trip you up. For anyone who is trying to solve a problem they feel is important, the act of trying to solve the problem is associated with a preferred picture of the future, which is vision.

Purpose has a catch; there's a twist and it's actually hidden in the definition. Here's a generic definition of purpose: Purpose is the reason for which something exists or is accomplished. This means purpose is a means to an end. We all know the analogy in sales of not selling the drill, sell the hole, and don't sell the newspaper, sell the news, don't sell the sausage, sell the sizzle. If you look at any product or service and say, what's the purpose of this product? The answer to this question is always a means to an end. And there's the catch.

Most people, from business owners to employees, are not willing to be a means to an end. Most of them want to be the end, and they want something else to be a means to their end. But if you're an end, you can't be a means to an end. This is why so many people resist the idea of purpose. They don't think of it in terms of creating a means to someone else's end.

When you commit to becoming a means to an end, you commit to something bigger than yourself, you can unlock purpose and build a business that scales into future generations.

STOP SELLING YOUR PRODUCTS AND SERVICES AND START SELLING YOUR PURPOSE

I hope you're getting the idea that purpose forms the core of everything we do and why and how we do it. Simply asking the question 'what is my purpose' is the wrong question, and that can lead you down the wrong path. I certainly understand why people ask it. We've all asked it, myself included. I'm sharing this with you today because I asked the wrong questions too. Let's explore….

What's behind the question, 'What is my purpose?'. In other words, you want to know your purpose so you won't be without purpose again.

'Why am I here?' - you want to know **why** you're here so you'll know **why** you're here. Even though these are not necessarily poor questions, I don't think they get us to purpose. I think it just brings us back to me and my end. My advice is this - as long as you're hung up on 'what is my purpose', and 'why am I here', you're probably not going to get there because purpose is about becoming a means to an end, a means to someone else's end.

WHAT'S A BETTER QUESTION?

Perhaps by suggesting those questions are the wrong questions, you may think I know the right questions. I don't think I necessarily know the right questions, but I can suggest better questions - questions that can lead you to your purpose. Rather than ask 'What am I here for?', you could ask yourself **'Who am I here for?'** Or, as you look at your team and your organisation, ask the question **'Who are we here for?'**.

If you've been following my blog, articles and posts for a while you will have heard or seen me discuss the importance of building authentic professional relationships and the social economic benefi s that can be unlocked through them. Like the catch in purpose, there's always been a catch in relationships. **That catch is self-interest**. If I'm more interested in what I can get from a relationship, that relationship will always struggle to be authentic and therefore is unproductive. Because purpose is a means to someone else's end, all the while you're thinking 'what's in it for me', you will struggle to unlock your purpose.

To really embrace a life of purpose, whether it's in the marketplace or the not-for-profit world, and to really stand out in an increasingly competitive world, you must accept that you need to move away from being an end and become a means to an end that is not you.

PURPOSE HAS A PRICE

Some of you may know that back in the 19th and 20th centuries, pharmacy and chemist shops sold a huge range of drugs designed to help people with their health problems. This included all manner of things which we have now found to be harmful, and the shops have subsequently stopped selling them. While I was researching this topic, I came across what I think is a great example of purpose having a price.

Larry Merlo is the CEO of CVS Pharmacies and in 2014, not that long ago, CVS became the first major pharmacy chain to stop selling cigarettes and some other tobacco related products. Many of us didn't know this happened. In fact, we go into pharmacies today and we know they don't sell cigarettes or tobacco related products. It never even crossed our minds that somewhere along the way, somebody took the first step, a decision to sacrifice profit for purpose. Larry's message was clear; **The sale of tobacco products is inconsistent with our purpose, because our purpose is to help people on their path to better health.**

Putting purpose ahead of profit initially cost them millions and they knew and planned for it. But Larry and the board decided that they wanted their company to embrace the idea of purpose, even though it cost them, they became a means to an end and the end wasn't all about them. Big decision. Other companies began to follow suit and now they've become an industry leader because people will always rally behind purpose over profit

PURPOSE IS THE PATHWAY TO MEANING

When an individual or a company embraces the idea of purpose, they become a means to an end. You cannot have meaning in life, or your organisation cannot have meaning in the marketplace, if you are not willing to become a means to an end beyond you or the organisation. When people say 'there has to be more to life than this', or they say 'there has to be more to growth in business than this', what they're really saying is there has to be more to life than me. Those who devote themselves to themselves, or an organisation that devotes itself to itself will ultimately have nothing but themselves to show for themselves. If it's all about the organisation, that's all they'll have to show for it.

When an individual or an organisation decides to do something that's not just about themselves, they will have more than themselves to show for themselves, and more than themselves to grow into future generations of their organisation.

I appreciate this idea may seem a bit tricky and you may think it unnecessarily complicated, but I hope you've followed this train of thought this far because you've bumped up against trying to find your purpose for yourself or your business and it's the catch in purpose that's getting in the way. We know everyone should embrace purpose, and there is a price and there is a cost, but the advantage and reward is meaning. You can't have meaning in life as long as it's all about you. Your business or organisation cannot have meaning in the marketplace if it's all about the business, who you are and what you're doing.

Think about how many times you've seen social media posts that are all about what someone has done or what they've achieved. Celebrating their own achievements rather than the achievements of those they serve. There's a saying I think is relevant here, and I can't remember from whom. It goes, *'If it doesn't matter when you're gone, it doesn't matter now.'* I think this has a lot to say about how much we have all become distracted by all types of media noise, and who can shout the loudest about their achievements. Anyway...

LET'S DISCUSS WHAT YOU CAN DO TO TAKE THIS IDEA FORWARD

Earlier I suggested better questions to ask yourself are, 'Who am I here for?' or 'Who are we here for?', and here are three additional points to help you move forward.

The first is - **Begin looking at everything you are currently doing through the lens of meaning.** You can start by asking yourself, 'Are you willing to pay the price to position your business or organisation to be more about purpose than just about the company?' By paying the price, I don't necessarily mean sacrificing profit as Larry and CVS did, but are you willing to invest to unlock purpose or are you happy to remain average. As I said earlier, those who devote themselves to themselves will ultimately have nothing but themselves to show for themselves. But if you devote yourself to more than yourself, you will ultimately have more than yourself to show for yourself.

WE LEARNED THIS FROM FUNERALS

A great funeral is when there's a life worth celebrating, and a life is worth celebrating when it's a life that was given away. The value of anyone's life is always measured in terms of how much of it was given away, but you don't give away your life until you're willing to become a means to an end. The eulogy never reads 'We're here to celebrate the life of xxx, he didn't really do anything but look after himself'. Now translate that into your organisation. When it's time to handover your business to future generations, what will you be remembered for - a life of leadership serving your team and clients, or a life spent serving the company.

As you begin looking at everything you do through the lens of meaning, look for the sizzle in every sausage!

The second point is to - **Pay attention to what stirs your heart**. What do you find yourself thinking about when you can think about whatever you want to think about. What leads you down the path of something that might take you beyond you, or set you up to be a means to someone else's end. In your business, what wrong are you trying to right, what injustice are the products and services you provide solving for others that create a means to their end.

Thirdly and arguably most importantly is - **Surround yourself with on purpose people.**

We all know the quote, "You are the sum of the five people you surround yourself with", but there's science behind it. Research published by Stanford Social innovation Review showed that when two people are in each other's company, their brainwaves begin to align.

The research goes on to say, *'that the more we study engagement between people, we see time and time again that just being next to certain people actually aligns your brain with them. Something happens in our brains to physiologically align ourselves with the people we're around ... the people you surround yourself with actually have an impact on your engagement with reality beyond what you can explain. And one of the effects is you become alike. Of course, this mirroring of unconscious behaviour works both positively and negatively.* **When you surround yourself with can-do people, you believe you can do too, and** when you surround yourself with people who won't do, you begin to believe you can't do.

By surrounding ourselves with people who embody the traits we prefer, over time we will naturally pick up these traits. Surrounding ourselves with on purpose people is actually a strategy. If we really are serious about getting to the place where we're willing to take the step and make a sacrifice to do something meaningful with our lives and build a meaningful purpose in our businesses that is not all about ourselves.

In the book *Dare to Serve* by Cheryl Bachelder, she says, 'The point of purpose is to determine how you will serve others' bottom line. If you don't have a plan to serve others, you don't need a purpose.'

I hope this article has brought clarity to understanding the catch in finding your purpose. I'll leave you with these final thoughts. Are you willing to serve others or just serve yourself and your organisation? Are you willing to be a means to an end that isn't you? If you are, you are on your way to embracing a life of meaning and purpose and if not, you're going to miss out. When you've retired from your role or company and people gather to celebrate your life, will they have a rich track record to celebrate, or will they have to 'make things up.'

Find out more about purpose by reading my other articles, and book a call with me to talk about the future of your business.

See also
How To Achieve The Second Goal Every Business Owner Wants (p1)
What Can We Learn From Not-For-Profit Organisations (p77)
The Five Most Important Things To Do When Creating A Team Skills Development Plan (p99)
Be, Do, Have - What Does It Mean (p107)
Five Top Tips For Managing A Growing Team (p229)

How To Get Recruitment Right First Time - Part 1

As you grow and scale your business or organisation, getting recruitment right can be a challenge, especially in the early stages of business development. It's getting increasingly difficul to attract quality candidates without offering budget-busting salaries and benefits packages. The days of simply posting a job advertisement and waiting for the phone to ring are gone, perhaps never to return.

Now is the time to change your approach and think about recruitment in a different wa .

HOW DO YOU ATTRACT CUSTOMERS TO YOUR BUSINESS?

You have developed a marketing strategy and sales funnel that brings you the right customers who are willing to pay for your products and services.

HOW DO YOU ATTRACT THE RIGHT CANDIDATES?

Do the same! Develop a meaningful vision and purpose that attracts candidates to your mission because purpose, belonging, social responsibility and ethics, are becoming more important to quality candidates than just money and benefits - note I said quality candidates there

Recruitment should be a strategy you plan for, not just a reaction to a demand on capacity in your business. Just like your marketing and sales, it's a key factor that ensures you outperform your competitors.

Here are six more things to include in your approach to planned recruitment.

RECRUIT PEOPLE WHO KNOW HOW TO TAKE THE POSITIVES FROM LIFE'S JOURNEY

We all know stuff happens in life. The right candidates are those who know how to find and apply the lessons learned from difficul experiences. Rather than blaming other people or external factors. They own and take responsibility for lessons learned and maintain an optimistic attitude and focus on what could be better. These are the people you want in your business. You can discover people's real drive at interview.

RECRUIT PEOPLE WHO ARE MISSION 'OBSESSED'

I'm sure you appreciate the importance of mission alignment in your recruitment activities, but have you considered mission 'obsession'?

Recruiting people who are aligned to your values, purpose, vision and mission is vital if you want the right people around you who will stay loyal. It's critical to maintaining quality of culture in every organisation.

Make sure you ask every person you interview what is their personal connection to your mission. You will very quickly discover who authentically lives and breathes your mission and is truly obsessed by it, and who is just saying what they think you want to hear.

Earlier I talked about purpose, belonging, social responsibility and ethics. This highlights an individual's personal mission 'obsession'. When your obsession is connected to theirs, you've found the right person. Again, interview is the best time to discover those who are mission 'obsessed'.

RECRUIT PEOPLE WITH SKILLS AND EXPERIENCE

You want to find people with the skills and experience needed to hit the ground running. Skills and experience are often emphasised first when recruiting and I have deliberately not put these first in this list of ideas as getting recruitment right first time in your business has to shift towards what's attractive to your candidates - and this is purpose, vision and belonging.

RECRUIT PEOPLE WHO MATCH YOUR BUSINESS STAGE

What are the risks to individuals and the business of someone from a different stage business joining you? For example, does your candidate understand what joining your business entails both for their personal life, their own money situation, and also in the way things are done.

If you have someone joining you because your vision is more attractive, perhaps from a larger company, they may be baffle by the fact that there are so few systems and processes in place that they're just going to have to get stuck in and do all sorts of different tasks. This can spark clashes between employees where someone didn't think it was their task to complete.

Because you get excited by hiring someone who's just come from a business at a different stage than you, you may think they're going to be incredible. If they don't understand the mindset shift that needs to happen when they join, there can be a feeling of disconnect which can easily be mitigated in advance when your candidate fully understands the implications of joining a different stage business.

Consider this question when recruiting - What stage of evolution has your business reached (are you an early-stage business, or is your business established and growing fast) and where are you going?

BEWARE THE INTERVIEW EXPERTS

Some people are very good at interviewing and not much good at anything else, and other people don't interview well but can do a great job. I have already talked about how you can discover the quality candidates you are looking for by asking about mission 'obsession', purpose, ethics, etc.

Here are three more things to consider before appointing a permanent post:

1. References - quality references that talk about work quality, how they work with others, not just "I've worked with this person for x years and they are great".
2. Task - a task you set them at interview to assess their capability and approach to work.
3. Probation period - where you and they have an effective weekly debrie .

GET BETTER ACCEPTANCE RATES WHEN MAKING OFFERS TO CANDIDATES

Now you have some new ideas about how to get recruitment right first time in your business. We have already talked about making your business more attractive to candidates in the same way as you do when marketing your products and services.

Write your offer letter in such a way that it prioritises who they are and what they want, not just ticking boxes of what you want. I know that may sound counter-intuitive, but the reality is it's a candidate's market, particularly because you are looking for quality. Include a compelling job specification your candidates will be proud to tell their friends about.

Instead of seeing recruitment as a process to run through to screen out bad candidates, you now have lots of new ways to get recruitment right first time and every time in your business. Apply the rule 'attitude before aptitude' and you won't go far wrong.

See also
How To Avoid The Catch When Finding Your Purpose (p11)
How To Get Recruitment Right First Time - Part 2 (p25)
What We Can Learn From Not-For-Profit Organisations (p77)
The 5 Most Important Things To Do When Creating A Team Skills Development Plan (p99)
Why People Leave People (p111)
What Does Packard's Law Teach Us About Business Growth? (p223)
Five Top Tips For Managing A Growing Team (p229)

Mark Jarvis

How To Get Recruitment Right First Time - Part 2

Growing your business with the right people can be a challenge, especially for early stage and high growth businesses. For many, finding the right people often starts with a wish list of characteristics, behaviours, skills, and experience, before soon realising they just can't afford their ideal candidate. They end up employing a person with perhaps 6 or 7 out of 10 from their perfect wish list.

It's not that the person is any less valuable, it's simply because the employer hasn't given enough thought to what they actually need. In this article, I'm going to explore some of the key points to think more closely about to help you get recruitment right first time. Do please also read Part 1.

This article is all about finding and hiring the best people for your company. It's a mixture of ideas because it's made up of my own experiences in finding the right people for my own businesses, what works, what doesn't, and the seismic shift in expectations that has occurred over the last few years.

There's one key point I think needs clarifying before we move on: the operational and cultural expectations of those you are recruiting. Here's why. When people move from a larger organisation to a smaller one, they sometimes do so because they want to feel more valued. The challenge in this situation is they will be used to a way of working that suits a larger organisation but not a smaller one. Helping them to shift and re-align to your way of working should be something you recognise and address.

Similarly, when someone moves from a smaller organisation to a larger one, it's sometimes because they are looking for a level of career progression not available in the smaller organisation. As well as the operational challenge noted above, there will be change in organisational culture your new employee hasn't experienced before which again, must be addressed early on to manage expectations and seamlessly integrate your new team member. Both these points are especially true for younger and high growth organisations, where the recruitment pool tends to be from the younger generations.

IT'S DIFFERENT FOR MORE ESTABLISHED ORGANISATIONS

Most people who lead more established organisations would like to carry on working the way they have traditionally done so over the last 20 years, but the cultural and operational expectations of your recruitment pool have changed dramatically, even more so since the global Covid-19 pandemic of 2020/2021. People want to work remotely, they want to work from home, they don't want to be in the offic more than a couple of days a week, if at all. It's enormously difficul to attract, onboard, train and develop a team of people when there's no one regular or daily point of contact that brings the whole team together. How do you train and mentor somebody when you're based in London, and the person you're talking to is in Europe or even further afield? This has been a major change and a major challenge, and I don't believe it will last successfully in its current format.

More and more of the more established and larger organisations are finding it increasinglly difficul to build cultures, and to mentor, lead and motivate teams of people when they don't see and meet them in person.

Managing people remotely is relatively straightforward when you already know them. Recruiting, mentoring, training, leading and motivating people is next to impossible when you're not starting from a place where those involved have developed a (professional) personal connection and relationship.

From a leader's point of view, especially in early-stage businesses where money is tight, what should you do if you're looking to grow a high performing team? What are some of the mistakes leaders make? What should you focus on and do first

Firstly, most people don't put enough effort and thought into the recruitment process itself. Most people who are asked to put a job specification together, especially a commercially focused role, will start by creating a tick list of the skills, strengths and attributes of the person they think they should be looking for. Because they haven't thought it through and they haven't considered whether they can actually get all those qualities in one person, and if they could, could they afford them, they end up settling for a 6 or 7 out of 10 from their wish list. I've learned that building a high performing team starts with clearly defining the role, both now and how the role will grow into the future.

Think about how you will go about finding the right person that matches the role that exists in the future and recruit someone who will grow into the role, both operationally and culturally. Stop recruiting for vacancies now, and start recruiting for the future. Work with an HR company, a recruitment company and a mentor who's been on the same journey.

Time and time again, I've seen leaders trying to recruit from their wish list without taking the advice of professionals early enough to get quality people, have proper profiles and specifiations written, and be realistic about what they are looking for. Not just that, but also making sure they can not only afford those people but can attract them. I have often sat in with my clients when they are reviewing candidates, selecting a short list for interview, then asking 'now you have your candidates, how are you going to attract them to join you?'

From what I see, most employers are still trying to balance the best skills and knowledge against a budget they can afford, without realising that finding the right people is as much about the candidate choosing you as you choosing the candidate. I've talked about the importance of building a recruitment in the same way as you do a sales in Part 1. The concept being that you invest in your sales pipeline and process, so do the same for your recruitment pipeline and process. You can never grow a business with the wrong customers, and you can never grow a business with the wrong people.

Have you ever spent time and money recruiting, only for the successful person to leave within a few months? Perhaps it's because you hadn't thought it through thoroughly enough.

The number of times I've seen an organisation hire the wrong person and waste three, six, or nine months because they didn't think it through properly in the first place is shocking. That's an expensive mistake to make, not just as a cost in time and money to the business, but also it's expensive culturally within their team, perhaps even expensive in terms of customer relations.

WHAT'S THE MOST DISASTROUS MISTAKE I'VE SEEN?

This is easy to answer - employing a friend and fitting the job role round them. When I say it out loud, it's laughable, but people still do it! I'm not saying never employ your friends, of course not, but if you do, do it by thinking it through thoroughly with a full job specification an role description. More importantly, think more about the future than what you think you need right now.

Jack has a business employing 22 people, it's a B2B service business in a high growth industry. As we've explored already, finding the right people fast enough can be challenging so Jack's answer was to reach out to his network and talk with his friends and colleagues. He even used the LinkedIn badge 'hiring'.

Needless to say, he received a great many enquiries and Jack thought, 'look at all these candidates, I'll be sure to find the right person here.' As he went through them, he found less and less had what he thought he needed. Berating his experience to his friends, one of them said, 'Don't worry Jack, I'll come work for you'.

Chris started work as Jack's operations manager in February 2022 and they both got on like a house on fire. As time passed, Jack began to find it difficul to increase productivity through Chris, and Chris managed the team's productivity through meetings and agendas rather than leadership.

It's easy to highlight these shortcomings in hindsight and all seemed fine until Jack came to work one day to find a resignation from Rachel. Rachel is one of Jack's longest serving employees and one of the key members of the team. What he subsequently discovered was that Rachel was finding it increasingly difficult not just to cope with Chris's management style, but also the seemingly flippant way Jack and Chris interacted, simply because they were such good friends.

Who was at fault, well perhaps both Jack and Chris. Jack because he hadn't thought through what he needed his operations manager to be, perhaps thinking that Chris is a great guy and I'm sure he'll be good at the job. Chris because he hadn't had the opportunity to understand the role completely, what Jack's expectations were and the importance of professional conduct.

When cultural excellence is challenged, the best people leave first.

Jack's lesson - don't skip steps in your recruitment process, even for a friend or colleague. Jack and Chris are still working together having learned from their mistakes, sadly Rachel has moved on.

My hard-learned lesson was this - don't risk the future of your business by settling for just some of your ideal candidate qualities, think about your vision and the future of the business, not just what's here now. With a focus on the future, you will be able to create a thoroughly thought through role description which is no longer simply a wish list but a fact list, and get some help to do it. This alone will help you take a massive step forward in attracting and retaining the right people.

LET'S EXPLORE THE ROLE COMPENSATION HAS IN RECRUITMENT.

Traditionally most organisations, especially early-stage, feel like they're caught between a rock and a hard place. They want the highest quality people for the lowest possible price. In recent years, there's been a shift towards additional forms of compensation, employee benefits packages for example. In addition to asking, 'What's the role?' 'Who will I be working with?' and 'Who will I report to?' candidates are asking about the package not just the salary. Perhaps it's part ownership, health and wellness benefits, discount schemes, etc

I think most businesses now offer some sort of care package or employee benefits package. By far the one that interests me the most is the concept of part ownership or shared ownership. As a way to attract the right people and retain them, offering a stake in the organisation and therefore the future success of what is now their organisation, can create a very strong productivity incentive and be naturally motivational.

How that might be structured in your organisation depends entirely on the size and set up you are building, but I've found this idea to be particularly attractive to the right people. Part ownership or stakeholder ownership is not a new idea, it's common practise in the legal and financial industries, so why not in your organisation too

NOW YOU HAVE YOUR SHORTLIST, WHAT'S NEXT?

Let's imagine you've come up with a shortlist of three, four or five really excellent candidates who meet the brief (as described above). What's the best way to go through and assess those candidates and attract the best one. I've found that it's vital to have a good process and to follow it with every candidate you bring through.

Firstly, I would recommend that you adopt some sort of psychometric profiling, not as a way to choose or exclude candidates, but as a way to understand how to best align them in your organisation. Understanding how people work and how they work with others is key to integrating them fully into your organisation. I profile everyone who comes into my businesses, and I do it to maximise my knowledge and information about those people, and it helps me to ask better questions.

I use them at the second or third interview because it gives us a really good understanding of what their drivers are and which team they're best suited to. If you've got someone who's strongly analytical and process oriented, then you'll engage them with more technical tasks. If they're very strong in terms of emotional intelligence, then you may find them better suited to customer facing activities. Please remember, this is about helping your recruits feel engaged and comfortable in their role, and fully integrated into your team.

So, the steps so far are:
- first inte view
- psychometric profil
- second interview
- third interview.

The next thing I do, particularly if they're going to be responsible for communicating a message about the company, which includes any customer facing role, is to give them some kind of presentation to do so that you know they can actually present, rather than fall over at the last hurdle or turn into a quivering mess in front of people. This is often delivered as part of the third interview. On occasion, depending on the role, I've also asked some of their future colleagues to attend too.

Next, I get them into a social environment by taking them out for lunch or arranging a small social gathering with colleagues, so I know how they behave. One of my clients recently chose not to make a job offer because the person was just a little inappropriate in a social environment and with potential colleagues to feel that person was the right person to uphold the organisation's culture both internally and externally. I'm sure you can see how behaviour affects culture, I would rather know sooner than when it's potentially too late.

A WORD ABOUT ARTIFICIAL INTELLIGENCE (AI)

If your recruitment process is just about filter ng CV's, or you're working from a database, or if you're using LinkedIn or job boards to find candidates, AI can do that. Yes, you'll be able to find people, but are they the right people who will engage and stay with you because they feel part of something.

At the core of every organisation are people and their relationships. I can't predict the future, what I do know now is AI can't build relationships and can never replace the human interaction between people talking with people. On the point of remote working, how can you have a cup of coffee with a colleague if you're not around them. How do you ask about taking Thursday afternoon off when the person you ask might be having the worst day possible and they're grumpy and angry? How do you pick your moments when you're not around the people who matter.

It's not that I'm not a fan of AI, I do believe it has a place, we must remember however that it's a tool not an answer. In terms of recruitment, there will never be a way to replace the opportunity to look someone in the eye and shake their hand. And, as discussed already, mentoring, training and leading people is just not possible if you've never met in person.

Let's summarise with these closing points.

1. Clearly define the type of person you want, not just for now, but into the future and get help to do it.
2. Have a process you follow no matter the candidate.
3. Use psychometric profiling to align recruits, not exclude them.
4. Check behaviour in a social environment and include your team.
5. Think about a compensation package which goes beyond what everyone else does.

Finally remember, the culture of your organisation is at stake. It's not just about growing your team and scaling your business, it's about creating something that lives and thrives beyond your tenure.

See also
How To Get Recruitment Right First Time - Part 1 (p19)
How To Leverage AI In Business (p35)
The Five Most Important Things To Do When Creating A Team Skills Development Plan (p99)
Why People Leave People (p111)
Five Top Tips For Managing A Growing Team (p229)

Mark Jarvis

How To Leverage AI In Business

Thus far I've resisted the temptation to write specifically about the use of artificial intelligence (AI) in our lives and in business, until now. I've been using AI for a while now (I'll explain how I use it later) and there is no doubt that it's here to stay. Now I want to share with you my own experiences and offer a perspective I hope will help you embrace AI and the wider use of technology to build greater efficiencies into your busines

The first sweeping statement I'm going to make is this - AI is in no way intelligent. It's just the application of incredibly fast processing power, brought to bear on publicly available information. AI cannot, at the moment, create anything new, it just trawls every piece of information available globally, and then presents it in a summary format.

WITH THAT IN MIND, WHERE DO WE BEGIN?

Let's begin with an example most people have experienced - time. Time is the most valuable asset we all have, and pouring resources into strategies that don't deliver results can be an expensive use of time. In fact, it's a waste of time and money. We also know growing a business is not just about making money, it's about improving the lives of the people we serve.

AI AND TECHNOLOGY CAN SAVE YOU TIME, WHEN YOU KNOW HOW TO USE IT PRODUCTIVELY

Productively doesn't mean typing a question into the AI platform and copy/pasting the output into your social media - something I see nearly every day - and it's becoming so easy to spot! Using AI productively means using it in the same way you would an intern, for research, for ideas, and for drafting, not for producing the finished product

Today we're not just talking about how to use AI in your business, I've actually talked to AI about business. As you already know and you're already thinking, this can be quite a polarising topic, depending on who you talk to. Some people see it as a tool for the future. Some see it as job threatening, and some see it as potentially harmful to society, you know, the 'Terminator comes true' scenario. What's undeniable is it's already having an impact on our lives, on our industries and on our businesses.

LET'S START BY TALKING ABOUT THE POTENTIAL OF AI IN BUSINESS

There was a recent article from Forbes that suggested artificial intelligence can be used to improve decision making for leaders in businesses. As a leader and business owner, you understand the importance of better decision making. We want our decisions to move us forward and not create regret for us or for our businesses.

Some people are really excited about the possibilities of AI, and some people are terrified. Some people just don't like that things are changing, and some people don't want to use it because they don't want to do something new. And then some people don't want to use it because they're actually scared of it.

Regardless of how you feel about AI, better decision making is something we can all relate to, no matter where you are in your career or in your life. The more decisions you are responsible for, the better you want to be at making them. The role AI has in this process is to give you access to a deeper level of information and to allow you to step out of your box and view your next decision from a different perspective. By analysing data from a variety of sources, **AI can help leaders identify patterns and trends they might not have otherwise noticed.** Ultimately, it can lead to more informed and strategic decision making, which can have a significant impact on organisational performance.

USING AI IS LIKE INVITING THE WHOLE WORLD INTO YOUR DECISION MAKING PROCESS

Rather than just asking one or two other people what they think, you have access to the combined experiences of the whole world through a deeper level of information, which will help you make better informed and more balanced decisions. That's something I think many of us hadn't even considered before.

AI IS AN ENHANCED VERSION OF GOOGLE

Google searching in the past has been great, and it's served its purpose well, but now you have the ability to use AI to collect data and answers and record what you were talking about, even when you revisit it a few days later, a week later, or even a month later. This feature alone can help you build a framework of information that can broaden the scope of your research, which means your decision making can be better. The ability of AI to record and keep your interactions can be really helpful if you work on multiple projects at once as it's easy to jump back and forth from project to project. This is a great example of how AI can improve productivity and efficien .

AI IS YOUR INTERN NOT YOUR BOSS

Like many, I started out using AI to just play around with, but I hadn't systemised its use in my business. I guess it became the latest shiny object to use. Like many, I soon realised it was just regurgitating the same old information, even if it were presented in a different way. The use of AI in my business, and I believe it should be in yours, is to work out how to use it to make your life more efficien and to improve your ability to work productively and get things done right. Use it as a tool for research and delegate information gathering to it in the same way as you might an intern in your business. Like an intern, it can be helpful in completing tasks, but it relies on your ability to feed it with the right information in order for it to do its job effectivel . It's not quite trustworthy enough to work on its own without oversight. So treat it like an intern, not your boss.

There are many different ways to use AI, my favourite is to use it while I'm brainstorming a project or researching a topic - this article for example - and working with my clients to show them how to brainstorm using AI. As I've mentioned already, the ability of the platform to record the history of all my interactions separately really helps me to bounce from one project to another quickly and efficient , and the information returned builds over time so I can easily scroll back for previous responses, further saving time and building efficien .

THERE ARE CLEARLY POSITIVES TO THE USE OF AI, BUT WHAT ABOUT THE RISKS

There are risks of course, the first and most obvious I think is industry related. If you have a business or a role that relies on the supply of information or knowledge for a fee, you are or will be under threat unless you adapt. How to do this is beyond the scope of this article but do give me a call if you want to know how.

The next risk is accuracy. You can't afford to spend time and money on a project based on inaccurate information. I'm an advocate of checking my own work, so I'm certainly not going to allow AI to give me information to send out into the world without reviewing it. Remember, treat it like an intern not your boss. As I've said already, AI generated copy is easy to spot, is it really worth your reputation for the sake of regurgitating the same old information as everyone else. Anecdotally, there is a story of a challenge to a legal case where the defendant relied on an entirely fictious precedent which had been generated by AI. Needless to say, the plaintiff won. The day AI begins telling us what it thinks we want to hear, will be our Terminator day...

There are many more risks of course, however, the final point I want to share is the danger of over reliance on technology to the point where it overrides our judgement or intuition. A point which I think we can all agree is what makes some leaders better than others. There's also a danger in using AI that you can lose that personal touch, the human connection that we all crave. I was having lunch just a few days ago with one of my clients, and we saw that someone had sent a shout out to someone else in their general Slack channel, it was so clearly written by AI that we both laughed and cried at the same time.

Think about this, the words were kind and it was accurate and on point, but we didn't take it as seriously because we knew it wasn't written by a person taking the time to share their personal feelings. The lesson to learn is if you don't want people to know it was written with AI, don't write it with AI. Or at least go in and edit it heavily and really adding your personal touch. Even though the message was real in the sense of it sounded good and it looked good, it still wasn't as sincere as something personal and makes a human connection.

Imagine this - your best friend's birthday is coming up and you go out to buy a card. You spend time looking through all the well-crafted greetings until you settle on one, perhaps it's perfect, perhaps it's as close as you can get to the message you want to share, so you go ahead and buy it. How often, when it comes time to write the card, do you add your own personalised message. I know I do! The messages in these cards are like AI, they may convey the message you want to give but are they truly personal.

Harvard Business Review has this to say about AI. I'm paraphrasing but it said - it's important to remember AI isn't generating new ideas, it's aggregating and predicting based on prompts. There's no new information, it's just taking all the information from the internet and spitting it back out to you in the way you want to see it.

A WHISTLE-STOP TOUR OF INSTAGRAM

I think most people are familiar with Instagram or the concept behind it, even if you don't use it. When Instagram came out, it was all about sharing a picture of your coffee or the sunset or whatever it is with people yoy know. That's where the app started.

Fast forwarding really quickly... After a few years, these people we now call influencers decided that they could use this app to make their life look perfect and a whole lot better and successful than it might actually be. So we saw a boom in influenc rs that were travelling and doing all these fun things which just made their life look like perfection. Not too much later an increasing number of people got tired of perfection. So a few of those influencers said what would happen if I actually started to share my struggles again, what happens if I actually start to open up to the reality of my life. They started sharing their struggles, their anxiety, their issues, the things in real life they were dealing with. **Those first influencers became heroes because people crave reality, and they crave imperfection.**

Bringing this back to the use of AI, I think as things become perfect, as copy becomes perfect, as marketing becomes perfect, and as strategies become more perfect because they're based on AI tools, people are going to crave human connection even more, and they're going to crave reality. I'm not saying it needs to be imperfect, of course not, but perhaps it does need to be vulnerable.

My point is, if creating perfect copy, perfect images, perfect marketing or perfect strategies through AI becomes too easy, human nature is going to crave something different. We are going to crave reality, we are going to crave the people connection.

Without distancing ourselves from new technology, we have to future proof ourselves against AI by cultivating human skills, emotional intelligence, interpersonal communication, things that are so important to the human psyche (which AI is going to make seem we don't need quite as much). I really think that's how you can future proof your job regardless of what you do. See, I did circle back and touch on the first risk I mentioned above... hope it helps.

SOME EXAMPLES OF AI IN PRACTICE

I started by asking, "Give me five things to do to grow my business." Here's what it came up with.

1. Increase your sales to existing customers
2. Attract new customers
3. Improve your products and services
4. Develop new products and services
5. Work with a mentor

There's a longer description of each and no, I didn't prompt the last one, it's what it returned.

I hope you can see there's nothing new there, and sharing this doesn't make me more clever or better in any way, it's just information freely available to you as well as me. What can make it truly useful is to add personal experiences and stories. Yes, I know AI can write stories but are they true. My point being we crave the human touch which AI cannot yet (if ever) provide.

Just to demonstrate a more complex enquiry, I thought I would ask it, "What's my scaling philosophy?" Here's what came back.

"Mark Jarvis is a business mentor, coach, and trainer who helps business owners and leaders to accelerate their growth and scale profitably. His philosophy about scaling businesses is based on his scaling formula: People x Processes x Planet x Products x Profitability = Sustainable Success. He believes that growing and scaling a business does not mean it has to be bigger, but it does need to be increasingly profitable. He also emphasizes the importance of authenticity, relationships, wellbeing, and social responsibility in business. He offers various programs, courses, and resources to help people grow and businesses scale."

Again, nothing new. It's information that's freely available from my internet presence, the difference is that it's been re-written in a summary format it thinks I want to receive.

GOOGLE VS AI

By 2004 Google was handling 200 million searches per day and it had revolutionised the way we searched for information. As we know, Google and other search engines index information from the internet and then represent it back to us using our website page titles and meta information, but it's still a straight copy of what we have already written. When we use Google, we are the ones that have to click the links, find, sort and read the information from each website, blog or resource. AI takes out the middle man by taking out the need for us to find, sort, read and summarise the information. **That's the step that can make us more productive and raise efficiencies in our businesses, and this, for me, is the essence of how to leverage AI in business.**

Footnote:

The Microsoft search engine Bing is already using AI (ChatGPT4) in this case, to provide more inclusive and comprehensive results. Here's the Microsoft marketing speel - *Chat, search and inspiration - all in one place with the new AI-Powered Bing. Dive deeper into subjects by typing follow up questions to get better answers, faster. Search That Gets You. Your Story, Your Search. The Answer Engine.*

Is this another nail in the coffin of traditional SEO, who knows.... What I do know is AI is here to stay and how we use it in our lives and businesses without losing the human touch is perhaps the biggest challenge we face.

See also
What Can We Learn From Not-For-Profit Organisations (p77)
The Key To Organisational Health (p93)

How To Spend Five Times Less Attracting New Business

Did you know that the majority of customers visit your website only once? Think about that. All the marketing efforts and money that is spent on driving traffi to your business results in most customers only giving you one chance. It can cost five times more to attract a new customer, than it does to retain an existing one.

Increasing customer retention rates by 5% increases profits by 25% to 95%, according to research done by Frederick Reichheld of Bain & Company.

With these statistics in mind, it makes sense to focus efforts and invest in relationships to nurture your existing customers, these people are spending their money on your goods or services, time and time again. This is not to say that you shouldn't market to new consumers, which is a must of course. Yet, these statistics can't be ignored.

Think carefully about how much time and money you are investing on acquiring new customers versus taking care of your existing customer base, building relationships and seeking referrals.

Start by engaging with your customers, suppliers and network via your social media channels.

How To Avoid Random Acts of Delegation

There comes a point for every business owner and leader when they have to admit, no matter how hard it is, they can't do everything, and they can't know everything. They know they'll have to delegate some responsibilities if they want their organisation to grow, scale and move ahead with increasing pace.

The ultimate goal for every business owner and leader is to **only do what only you can do**, which means you must stop trying to do everything and stop doing all the things you shouldn't be doing.

DELEGATION ISN'T AN EXCITING WORD

The topic of delegation makes most people groan, it's something we all know we need to do and get better at, yet most people don't really know what it means beyond giving tasks to others.

Delegation, when done right, is a **leadership development strategy**. Leadership development is not about sitting is a classroom every Tuesday morning, attending a workshop or going on a course. It's about demonstrating leadership skills to others to empower them to become better leaders than you or I. When delegation is done right, it really is a leadership strategy because you find out quickly who are the responsible leaders and who you can trust with increasing responsibility.

As leaders, and by leaders, I mean everyone with a leadership role, which includes you even if you are just leading yourself, we often get stuck because we know how we want things done and we know when we want things done. As we are responsible by nature, the idea of handing over responsibility is not intuitive. Refusing or denying your duty to hand over responsibility **puts a lid on your own leadership journey which ultimately puts a lid on the ability of your business or organisation to grow and scale.**

Sometimes we're hesitant to hand over responsibility because we want it done when we want it done, and it takes longer to explain to someone how we want it done than it does doing it ourselves. This creates a real danger of building an organisation that, as Jim Collins calls it, has a culture of "*…a genius with 1000 helpers*". Everything starts to hinge on a singular source of brilliance or talent. Truly great organisational leaders, even talented ones, avoid that by handing over responsibility through delegation.

Most of what I have learned has been through trial and error, mostly error, especially in the beginning. When I first started delegating to others as my team grew, it was by simply giving tasks to others to complete and being involved in all the decisions, because I believed it was necessary for me to be involved in everything up front. **What I didn't recognise was this was just delegating tasks and not delegating responsibility.**

One of the things I experienced that many of you may be experiencing now is: in the beginning, it's your responsibility to establish culture, which means you have to be a part of everything, but you can't be in everything for very long without destroying the culture at the same time, because the goal is to **create a culture of leadership.**

I learned by pushing responsibility as far down the organisation as possible began to create that culture of leadership which meant my business could grow and it wasn't being held back by the 'genius at the top'.

HOW TO BUILD A LEADERSHIP DEVELOPMENT STRATEGY THROUGH FOUR LEVELS OF DELEGATION

Delegation is critical to personal health, organisational growth, and is the balance point between micromanaging on one end and the complete abdication of leadership on the other end. **Random acts of delegation won't cut it** if you are to become a leader of leaders. By this I mean delegating without clarity, where expectations are not clear, not because the individual doesn't have the ability or desire to do well, but because they are not clear on how to succeed. Remember, this is not about what success in completing a task looks like, that's just management, **this is about success in responsibility**.

Here are the four levels of delegation as I've discovered them.

1. Investigation
2. Informed progress
3. Informed results
4. Ownership

Let's explore these levels one at a time. First a note for all my readers - I'll do my best to explain these concepts as clearly as I can based on the space we have here, but if you really want to explore the comprehensive application of these principles in your organisation, get in touch for a chat.

Before I unlocked the concept of delegation as a leadership development strategy, I was doing what most do and expanding my business through employment and management. I was beginning to feel overwhelmed because I was involved in everything, and stagnation was beginning to creep in because I couldn't grow beyond what was around me in the moment. I read everything I could read on leadership which included the topic of delegation and sat in a few classrooms. I came across lots of different pieces of information from different places and pulled it together to create these four levels of delegation.

LEVEL 1: INVESTIGATION

This level is almost a pre-delegation level. In some ways investigation is when you ask a prospective leader not necessarily to make a decision, but just to get information so that you both can collectively make a decision that supports a project or leads to a task or action at some point. This level is about delegating research - the opportunity for someone to gather information so the larger team can make a better decision.

This is a good way to measure a person's capability without risking too much. **Remember, this is not about getting a task done, this is about owning responsibility.**

WHY THIS IS HELPFUL

It's perfect for giving aspiring leaders an opportunity to contribute to the overall goal and to the bigger team. At the same time, we're not burdening them with a massive task they're not quite ready for. Allowing them to investigate and come back with recommendations and information really is helpful for them.

Imagine you're thinking about launching a new project. Before any decision is made to launch or not launch, there are lots of things to discover; costs, resources, how many people need to be involved, supplies, delivery etc. These are activities you can delegate before making a decision. A great way to engage the people you may have in mind to lead the project and involve them as early as possible because **this step creates a sense of ownership with a team before you hand over the actual responsibility.**

I used to think delegation had to be specifically tied to an individual task or a project, the reality is that we can back delegation up further and bring more people into the process at the same time as growing future leaders by demonstrating best practice, all before you even get to decision making. This explodes one of the typical myths around delegation because when we hear the word delegation, we picture the boss or the leader calling someone into the offic and saying, "I have an idea, I have a project, I have a task for you to complete, off you go..." What I'm proposing is that effective delegation (leadership) begins before that by saying I'm asking you to take responsibility for this information gathering activity, not simply to jump in and complete the task.

LEVEL 2: INFORMED PROGRESS

This is where we really ask someone to own an activity, but there's more to it that just delegating responsibility. **Remember, we're demonstrating to future leaders how they can become better leaders themselves through best practice.**

Informed progress means they come back to you with regular updates throughout the activity, task or project, and then to let you know when it's completed. You are remaining available for the duration, but you're not releasing them to take care of it completely on their own. **You are asking them to own it, but to also keep you informed along the way.**

A good example of this is something I did in the second business I started. Why not my first business? I hear you ask, because I hadn't learned about the relationship between effective leadership and delegation then. My second business was in property development, essentially buying, refurbishing and selling residential properties. As we grew, I was considering moving into building not just refurbishing homes so I set one of my team, Ben, the task of finding out what it would take to launch this arm of the business - this is covers Level 1: investigation.

Having shown his competency through the research and information gathering stage, I then gave him ownership of the project by positioning him with a Level 2 delegation. This was especially effective as he had been involved from the initial idea and was very motivated to succeed, far more than just giving him the project with no prior involvement. Ben had complete control, and more importantly responsibility for the project, he could 'borrow' staff from other projects, appoint suppliers and manage finances, he truly owned the project and I have to say, he was brilliant.

I was kept informed via our project update meetings every two weeks, keeping me up to speed on progress and giving him increased confidence in his abilities

WHY WAS THIS HELPFUL

Because Ben was involved from day 1 of the idea, when I called him to ask him to own and take responsibility for the project, it wasn't a surprise. Our conversation didn't start with 1000 questions about what, how, why, where, etc. It started with Ben saying "I'm so glad you asked, I've been itching to get the go-ahead". **Think about that next time you launch a project and have to start with a half-day team briefing and Q&A.**

Because I had involved Ben from the start not the launch, I had already got a sense of whether or not he wanted to do it, and whether or not he could do it. He had a sense of whether or not he wanted to do it, and whether or not he could do it. This way you're a long way down the road by the time you finally hand over responsibility. For leaders who are constantly thinking about the future, we're often a little bit tight with information and **we sometimes skip that first step which makes the second step so much more complicated than it needs to be.**

THERE'S A CATCH

How did I give Ben ownership and responsibility without it feeling like I was micromanaging.

Having an update meeting every two weeks could easily have made Ben feel like I was micromanaging and checking up on him. It all comes down to how you hold those meetings.

Micromanaging for me has always been about telling people how to do a task. Level 2 delegation is not about telling them what to do or how to do it, it's just asking them to keep you informed as they do it. This approach is simply sharing information between equals and not reporting to the boss. Of course, challenges and problems occurred along the way, and Ben knew I was always available should he want to ask for help, but **our regular meetings were not focussed around Ben asking what I thought he should do next**. If he did need to ask, we had agreed that he would present the problem, the choices to solve the problem, which choice he had made and why, (and the outcome - Level 3 more on that next). It was never about Ben asking for permission to act, it was done already. For entrepreneurial leaders, this is sometimes hard to swallow because we already find it hard to let go, but if you are going to build a successful and productive high-performing team, you must delegate ownership and responsibility.

I have lost count of all the mistakes I have made so it's unreasonable of us to expect others to not make mistakes too. Remember, this is as much their learning journey as it is yours.

ONE FINAL POINT BEFORE WE MOVE ON TO LEVEL 3

How often should you hold these update meetings. Every project, task and circumstance is different of course, what I will say is that saying "if you need anything, just ask…", effectively leaving your prospective leader on their own won't work because you don't know what's going on and they don't feel supported and **that's not the best practice you want others to copy**. They key is to hold regular scheduled meetings that are planned, structured and focussed.

Remember, this is about giving your future leaders the clarity and pathway to learn and succeed.

LET'S RECAP SO FAR

The first level of delegation, investigation, means I just want you to go and do some research, not to start any projects yet. Don't accomplish any tasks, just gather information, bring it back to me or bring it back to our team, then we can decide what to do next. Then Level 2, informed progress. Informed progress is a little bit bigger, a little bit more in depth than investigation. Informed progress means I have a project for you to own, but as you accomplish it, I just want you to keep me informed through regular meetings so I can stay updated but also so I can stay available to help you through the process, not to micromanage it, but just to be available to understand what your needs are and to understand how I can help you accomplish it.

LEVEL 3: INFORMED RESULTS

Informed results is the next level for a leader to not just own and give updates of a project or task, but to do it exactly the way they feel and then to let you know when it's done. You're not going to meet all the time and talk though progress, you just want to know when it's accomplished. You may ask what was done when it's accomplished, any problems along the way or an overview of the timeline, but you have given your leader ownership, responsibility and permission. **This is the lesson you want them to learn so they demonstrate this framework to others and the organisation grows with a culture of leadership.**

The reporting process for Level 3 is all about evaluating and reviewing results and taking the learnings forward to build increasing performance and productivity.

As an entrepreneurial leader myself, I know from experience how hard it can be to let go without micromanaging. **That's why these 4 levels are a leadership development strategy for you as much as for your team.**

LET'S POP BACK INTO BEN'S STORY

Ben and I had been working together at Level 2 (informed progress) for about 6 months and the first newly built property was about to be handed over to the estate agent for sale. Remember, the Level 2 step is all about progress. What happened, what problems there were, the options for a solution, and what was done. The Level 3 step, whilst similar, is separate because it's not about progress, it's about results.

Here's a good example of the difference.

If you've ever been involved in property development, even building an extension to your home, you will know how often snags and delays crop up. As we were building properties, we often came up against snags, amendments and queries from the planning regulator, which sometimes had to go back to the architect to then be resubmitted for approval. Because Ben and I were now working in a Level 3 leadership relationship, our now monthly meetings simply reported on the result of what was done, why, and what the outcome was. We were talking about what happened, not what was happening. It's a subtle step but really important if you are going to truly be able to move to Level 4.

The goal was to make sure Ben felt he owned his leadership journey and that what he was learning was percolating through his team too. By giving Ben ownership of the results, we're moving towards Level 4.

LEVEL 4: OWNERSHIP

Ownership means that you have delegated everything about a project or task. You don't need regular updates and you don't need to meet regularly. You'll remain available if they need to ask questions, but you're going to schedule those times because, like Level 3, **query meetings are scheduled in advance and not based on urgency**. I know what you're thinking…."what if something happens and they need to call me". What I hope I've shown you is that by following these levels, your leader has proved their capability to make decisions both to you and to themselves. Of course, if there is a crisis, there's always a pathway up the chain, but make sure it's only used for a genuine crisis.

Now working at Level 4, Ben and I, together with other project leaders discussed results and learnings, reviewing performance, and planning future growth strategies at our monthly board level meetings. Ben was motivated because what he was doing and it was truly his project. What had become a new arm of the business he had taken responsibility for because he had been involved from the very first idea

I hope these 4 levels have given you a framework for your own leadership development as well as a way to inspire future leaders in your own business.

One of the biggest mistakes I see business owners making is to jump straight to a Level 4 delegation and then try to keep their people motivated to perform. I call this a random act of delegation because you have a task that needs doing and you just give it to the person you think could do it without any real planning - my experience has shown me it just doesn't work this way. If you're serious about building a high-performing team do what I've shared with you here and drop me a line for a chat - it's already hard doing what you are trying to do, help may just make your own journey easier and faster.

SOME ADDITIONAL NOTES

What happens if at some point you recognise that something isn't working? Yes, I have had to jump in on occasion, but in all honestly, I've only had to do that because I hadn't followed these 4 levels. The problem wasn't the person, it was because I hadn't positioned their leadership development journey correctly. I wasn't clear, I didn't set up specific expectations, or I didn't define success well enough. There have been times when I've stepped in and the person was shocked because the way they were measuring success was different to the way I was measuring success, that was my fault not theirs. I do think as leaders, at some point we have to look in the mirror before we step in, and take responsibility ourselves before taking a task away from someone.

Level 1 is about assessing competency, deciding if I think they are capable, and if they want to do it. This is the same for the leader, do they think they can and want to do it. When you find the right people, and take them on a leadership development journey, you are developing their skills and knowledge in a far better and more practical way than sitting in a classroom and learning theory. They are significantly less likely to fail when they own and take responsibility for their own success. Yes, mistakes will be made, it's how you recover and learn which makes the difference

RECOGNITION

As we delegate responsibility for projects, it's all too easy to let what others are doing slip from our mind. My key learning was to always recognise people for their contribution not just their success. **Make a point of catching people in your organisation doing extraordinary things**, say thank you to the person, their manager, and their leader. Make your gratitude intentional rather than just accidental.

Remember to get in touch for a chat and get some help with your own leadership development journey - unless you'd rather sit a classroom...

See also
How To Get Recruitment Right First Time Part 1 (p19)
How To Get Recruitment Right First Time Part 2 (p25)
How To Unlock The Power Of Focus (p85)
The Key To Organisational Health (p93)
The Five Most Important Things To Do When Creating A Team Skills Development Plan (p99)
Five Top Tips For Managing A Growing Team (p229)

Why Start-ups Sometimes Fail

Most start-up business owners soon realise that gaining traction in the early years is hard, and its true. There are however, things you can do to make it simple, and today I want to share with you two principles that if not understood and overcome, can become a blockage to growth, even increase the likelihood of failure.

If you want to grow your business at the rate you want to grow it, in an industry where your competitor landscape is getting increasingly complicated, you must embrace technology, social responsibility and sustainability or you will end up losing opportunities to others who are. You need to hire faster and smarter in those areas because you know you now have what's called a 'product market fit'. The market needs the product, you have proved it and you have 100+ customers. Now it's a matter of expansion, and this usually requires some investment.

Expansion and growth happens about two to three years in, but in the early days, it's survival mode all the way trying to keep your head above water, invest and grow all at the same time as finding your feet as a business owner.

The first problem is this - because you are creating something nobody has fully accepted, you struggle to gain clients beyond the first flourish. It's like being the first to own a new iPhone. There are people who would stand in line all day to get one, those who must have the latest and newest thing, those are the early adopters.

Once you're done with early adopters, what do you do and how do you get to the mass market. This takes time and investment, but the mass market is where you start to become profitable.

First year start-ups, and anyone else who hasn't done this yet and is stuck, your focus should be on 'problem market fit'.

There are two distinct principles here, one is a 'problem market fit' and the other is a 'product market fit'. The first year of every start-up is, or should be, focussed on 'problem market fit', which means that you ask the question **does your market care about the problem you're solving?** Many start-ups fail because they assume that the market needs their product. The reality is your products could and probably will change, most younger businesses find their products and services changing quickly in the early years, mine did. I set out like many, by thinking that something I was good at would make a good basis for a business. Whilst that's true to a certain extent, I missed that I should have focussed on refining the problem I solved, not refining the product I offered. **When you focus on the problem you solve, you're not tied to the product, so innovation and development becomes easier.**

The first year in business is all about solving your 'problem market fit' and this doesn't require a lot of capital. It requires a lot of focus on the right problem, but then in the second or the third year, if you're doing everything right, you get to a point where you figure out what the real product is. Now you're focussed on the 'product market fit'.

I hope you can see the difference because many mix these two principles up, they swap them around because they fall in love with their product, or the idea of the product, so much they forget they're solving a problem. They sometimes believe it's all about them because they love what they do so much it becomes hard to hear someone say "that's not what I want", they then begin to think "you should want this thing, why you don't want it". It took me a long time to recognise it doesn't matter if I like it, what matters is, **have I clearly defined the right problem for the right market right now.**

Perhaps this explains why many start-ups never get past their love of their products and reach a plateau they just can't seem to break through, even if they are cash rich or have capital investment.

Like many, when I started out on my business journey, I started with a great idea and the drive to make it work. I think it's vital that we take a moment to think about the personal impact of starting a business. My decision to start a business was made following a long discussion with my wife about what we wanted to achieve in life and for our growing family.

What I missed was not putting a timeframe and milestones in place. It was like asking my wife to hold a heavy rock without telling her how long she needed to hold it - to carry the financial and emotional burden of starting a business without knowing if or when success would come. It took me nine years to grow and sell my first business, most of those years were profitable of course, but it took me too long to get started because I didn't tell my wife how long she needed to carry this heavy rock, which in turn perpetuated the belief that if I just kept doing more and working harder, it would all work out in the end. Thankfully it did, but I sacrificed a lot along the wa .

WHY SHARE THIS?

Simply this. I started by falling in love with the products I sold, it became all about the products and I became tied to those products. It was difficul to develop and innovate and let go of those products if they weren't right for the market. I missed that **starting up is all about 'problem market fit' not 'product market fit'** which meant growth was delayed.

Sometimes start-up businesses fail because it becomes too hard on them and their family or their cash reserves, and patience runs out before they reach the tipping point where they become profitable. This is as much true for small and medium businesses as it is for start-ups.

Of course, hindsight is a wonderful thing and now I've learned how to start, grow, scale and sell businesses, it's easy for me to make the points I have today. I hope you can take this concept of 'problem market fit' and make it a priority in your business before it's too late as statistics show that six in ten of start-up businesses do fail in their first five year

If you want some help clarifying the problems you solve for your markets, or would like to talk with me about any aspect of business, get in touch for a chat.

See also
How To Avoid The Catch When Finding Your Purpose (p11)

Getting The Business Basics Right
8 Tips For Success

Growing a business can be a complex and multi-faceted process, but there are some general strategies you should remember to help your business grow sustainably and profitabl .

Here are some reminders of the basics:

Develop a clear vision and mission for your business. Having a clear understanding of what you want to achieve and why you're in business can help you stay focused on your goals and help you make informed decisions about how to allocate your time and resources. A clear vision, mission and purpose will also ensure you build your team with the right people.

Identify your target market and understand their needs. Knowing who your ideal customer is, what they want and need from your business and the problems you solve for them, will help you tailor your products or services to better meet their needs and create more effective marketing and sales strategies.

Invest in marketing. Everything starts with your marketing strategy. Without a strategy and plan there will be no customers, no revenue and no business. Invest for success is something I learned early on, and get help to do it. You're great at what you do and others are far better than you could ever be in this vital area. Even if you're in the marketing industry, still get help. A fresh set of eyes makes a big difference

Build a strong online presence. In today's digital age, having a website and social media presence is essential for any business. Make sure your website is well-designed, easy to navigate, and provides clear information about the problems you solve, and your products or services. It's vital that your message is consistent across all platforms, including your staff LinkedIn profiles. Use social media to engage with customers, share news and updates, and promote your business.

Focus on customer service. Providing excellent customer service can help you build a loyal customer base and generate positive word-of-mouth referrals. Make sure your staff are well-trained and empowered to handle customer enquiries and complaints in a timely and professional manner.

Focus on recruitment. Finding and keeping the right people will be key if you are going to grow and scale your business. As well as your business plan and marketing plan, develop a recruitment plan so you can recruit early rather than when you need to. This will allow you to grow into your future rather than wait for it to happen.

Continuously innovate and improve. To stay ahead of the competition and meet changing customer needs, it's important to continuously innovate and improve your products or services. Keep an eye on industry trends, embrace technology and seek out feedback from customers to identify opportunities and areas for improvement.

Manage your finances effectively. Good financial management is critical to the success of any business. This includes creating a budget, tracking income and expenses, managing cash flo , and monitoring KPI's such as profit margins and return on investment. Make sure you have a solid understanding of your business's financial health, EBITDA, and work with experienced financial professionals to help you make informed financial decisions.

Remember, **growing a business takes time, patience, commitment and persistence**. Don't be afraid to experiment with different strategies, ask for help, and be willing to adapt and pivot as needed to achieve your goals.

Please also remember these are just the basics, there are tens of other things to consider if you want your business to build and scale.

See also
How To Get Recruitment Right First Time - Part 1 (p19)
How To Get Recruitment Right First Time - Part 2 (p25)
Why Start-Ups Sometimes Fail (p57)
Why People Leave People (p111)

The Tale Of The Wise Man

Once upon a time there was a wise man who shared his wisdom with all those who asked him. Sometimes the people who asked for help complained about the same problems and blamed others over and over again.

One day the wise man decided to help the people in a different way, so he told them a joke and all the people laughed.

The next time someone came complaining about the same problems, the wise man told the same joke again, this time the people didn't laugh as much. This happened a third time, so the wise man told them the same joke again, and this time no laughter at all.

The wise man smiled and said - you can't laugh at the same joke over and over so why are you always complaining about the same problems and expecting a different outcome

The moral of the story, next time you find yourself bumping up against the same or similar problems, focussing and blaming factors you cannot control, or find yourselves being held back by what's happened in the past, make a positive change and get help because what you keep doing is not solving the underlying problems.

Why Creative Distraction Is Holding You Back

One of the things we all have in common is we are all very easily distracted, and the things we get distracted by are never as important as the things we get distracted from.

I'm sure you know what I mean - you're working on a task and suddenly your phone beeps because you've received a notification. You wonder what the notification is for, so you pick up your phone and take a look. Perhaps you're working on your task and your email pings. So you stop what you're doing to check if it's something important or urgent. We've all done it, myself included. I often wonder when in our world we changed from focussing on what **we decide is important to being distracted by what others think we should find important.**

Did you know the first social media platform to reach 1 million subscribers, (and reached that point in 2004!). Now, decades later, we live our lives connected to it and, for many, at the expense of living a life. I'm not saying stop using social media etc, it's a big part of our modern world, I'm just saying there's a reason more and more people are tired of the doom and gloom spread by the press, and more and more people are turning off their notifications. **We are a social species, not a social media species.**

One of the biggest challenges you face as a business owner, leader or manager is avoiding what I call creative distraction. This is when you come up with an idea, or someone presents an idea to you, and you go off and research all of the different things you could do to implement the new idea. You may be thinking, well that's the whole point isn't it - **innovate, plan, implement**. Yes, but here's the problem.

Most get tied up in the idea and distracted by the activity rather than remembering that what's important is moving towards your vision. You may think you are working creatively on your business by going on a new course or workshop, writing a new blog or social media post, or re-writing your website, when in fact, you are just being distracted by what's immediate rather than what's important.

Of all the multiple things that fill our days, some are of course, marginally important. They're not bad things, but they're never as important as the things we get distracted from. I think it's fair to say that losing focus in some areas of our lives is not that big a deal. But there are certain things that if you take your eye off the ball, you wake up five years down the road and you realise; "Oh no, how did I get here? Where has the last five years gone?", and more importantly, "Why am not further forward than I expected or hoped for?" **"How did I end up on this track that I never remember choosing?"** Perhaps there's something that needs more of your undivided attention than simple day to day distraction or what others tell you should be important.

DON'T LET WHAT'S URGENT DISTRACT YOU FROM WHAT'S MOST IMPORTANT

Every day there's urgent stuff, whether it's a family or health matter, a client deadline or a task that must be completed. Remember what's important is where you're going not what's here and now. Of course manage the here and now, but keep focussed on what's important.

Whenever you are tempted to opt for immediate over ultimate, or want now over value most, or opt for optional over what's essential, you are choosing to change your priorities from what's important to what you perceive is urgent.

The nature of my work means I come into contact with people just like this. They have prioritised what they believe is urgent, perhaps they are chasing sales, perhaps trying to recruit, perhaps there's a gap in the management or leadership structure, perhaps communication is breaking down, or systems are slipping. What this almost always looks like is busy people constantly being distracted by what's urgent in their day-to-day lives and businesses, and forgetting what's important. **When you focus on what's important, what's urgent often goes away.**

How many times will you choose to work late, or extra hours to get a job done when your priorities are waiting for you at home. Something I did many years ago (read my story) before I realised what's important is how I live my life and share in the lives of those around me. Yes, I have started, grown and sold multiple businesses, but this one lesson many years ago has meant I'm focussed on what's important.

Think for just a minute about what is most important to you right now in your life. It may be a who or it may be what. Now I want you to think about your biggest distraction from the thing that's most important to you. Now let's ask the pinnacle question; **Why should I choose to stop working on what's most important to me, to start working on something that's less important?** Why should I choose to be distracted from my journey, vision and plan, just because it may bring a short-term win. Why would I do that?

WHAT'S THE DIFFERENCE BETWEEN A SCHEDULING CONFLICT AND A PRIORITIES CONFLICT?

We all have days where we just seem to be tripping over our diary with meetings that overrun, events we think we should attend but just can't quite seem to fit it in, then there's the day-to-day fire-fighting staffing customers, suppliers, delivery and supply chain issues. It's too easy to get bogged down in day-to-day urgency, as we have discussed already, and miss what's important. **Urgency tends to live in scheduling conflicts when you are not in control of your diary, and your most important things live in priority conflicts when you've lost sight of where you're going.** What are your real priorities?

You can always find time to put the wrong thing in your diary. You can always find time to squeeze something in that takes you away from what's most important to you. This is the essence of creative distraction.

What's your top priority, what's the number one thing you are not willing to compromise or be distracted from and don't trade ultimate for immediate. What is the thing you have to stay focused on until it changes. Whether it's your whole journey or whether it's a chapter in your life? Maybe it's a habit you finally need to break. Maybe it's a business you know you need to take to the next level. Maybe it's a relationship you need to rebuild.

While we're on the topic of relationships, here's a difficul question, but I have to ask it.

Who do you need to step back from? Who do you need to remove from your schedule to let others help and support you to your next level. Who is keeping you from becoming who or what you want to be. They're just not a good influence on you, because they're not going to help you get to where you ultimately want to be.

Think about these questions and points I have raised here. I hope they have allowed you to think differently about your priorities. There are many things you will do this year, and there are many things you can do this year. But **what is the one thing you must do this year, and are you willing to stay focussed on it until the task is complete and not suffer from creative distraction?**

See also
The Key To Organisational Health (p93)
Possibilities And Probabilities (p133)
What Are Big Goals And What Are Ordinary Goals? (p129)
What Does Making Changes In Business Really Mean? (p163)

Mark Jarvis

The Secret to Cultural Success in Business

I would like to share with you what I believe every business or organisation needs to know about culture. Of course, there are many ways to look at this topic and much has  been written, so here we are going to explore what are the most important things to think about or focus on that are within your control.

We can't control the marketplace, and nobody saw a virus coming that impacted our whole world, they are things out of our control. What are the things that any business CAN control.

- What does it take to launch a successful start-up?
- What does it take to grow beyond feast and famine?
- What does it take to scale through adversity?
- What does it take to make sure you don't plateau and get stuck there?

In a word, culture. I'm not talking about beanbags, pool tables and thumping music, I'm talking about what really matters personally and professionally.

This, I believe, can be summed up in three words.

MISSION, PEOPLE, AND CULTURE

Do you have a mission that you and everybody around you believes in, no matter what happens that's out of your control, even if it's a pandemic.

Are you hiring the right people? I'll simply say, your people, including yourself, are at the core and foundation of every business or organisation, no matter it's size or age. Until you have the right people, and your people are in the right place to grow and change, your business cannot adapt and scale.

Do you have a winning culture? I'm not talking about doing more, more leads, more sales, more customers, more time back, more money etc. I'm talking about the feeling of winning that everybody strives for, whether they know it or not, **when you feel like you've done better today than yesterday**. Is your pathway and purpose clear, do you know why you are doing what you do? Do you know how to make it better? Do you genuinely look forward to engaging in a productive workday?

When your mission is clear and you live it every day and when you are hiring the right people because you can (not because you must) and you have a winning culture, you have the seeds of success. Like any seeds, you must continue to water them, feed and nurture them so they can grow strong roots that cannot be blown over in the wind or affected by things out of your control

LET'S DIG A LITTLE DEEPER INTO WINNING

Winning is something we talk a lot about in business, but it's not all about making more money, of course, increasing revenue and profit is important, but it's not the only thing. Winning may be the feeling you get when you are making better appointments, not just closing the deal. It may be the feeling you get when you save some time for a customer, it may be a new initiative, product or service that makes people think about your brand. Whatever the win is, you must continually define and develop it because if you don't, someone else will, whether it is a team member defining their own win, or you just going through the motions having lost sight of your purpose.

What I see happening, especially in the early years of a business, is the beginnings of a sales culture where it's all about gaining more customers and getting bigger. Where the only focus seems to be on revenue. If that's not happening, then the perception can be you're not winning as a business. You can begin to think if you have money coming in, then you know you're growing. Everything feels good because you feel like you're winning the business game. Then, at some point, you're going to hit a plateau that you just cannot cross, that you just cannot seem to move beyond.

IT FEELS LIKE SOMEBODY JUST PULLED THE PLUG

Even though the organisation is successful, revenue is increasing, and the team is expanding, it still feels like you've reached a plateau you just can't seem to break through. Why? Because winning has become about growth. **By re-defining the win in terms of culture, you will be able to move beyond your plateau.**

HOW TO SCALE BEYOND YOUR PLATEAU

Many years ago, I remember a conversation I had with my coach, and it had such an impact on me it has stayed with me, and a principle I share with you here. I started my first business way back in the 1990s, and despite challenges and setbacks, it grew. We gained more customers, closed more sales and continued to grow - all good right?

Because I had done what most do, closed more sales, expanded the team because of demand, and overcame challenges when they occurred, winning became all about growth.

What happened then, which is easy to see now I look back, was that sales plateaued. What I mean by that is you cannot increase your sales beyond your capacity, that's why I hired more people. I call it 'Time Limited Turnover' or the entrepreneurs second see-saw.

I remember the day vividly when my coach said to me, "You keep talking about growth and quantity at all costs, how tall do you want your children to be? At some point growth reaches maximum and you need to change your focus." All I had done up to then was focus on growth and at some point, growth plateaus. Once your children have grown as tall as they are ever going to be, you must work out how to multiply and scale.

Whatever your industry, business or organisation, whatever size, age or stage you have reached, figuring out how to create a culture that's winning, and **continually redefining the win within the rhythm of your business, is the key to your future success**. If it's all about more sales (or anything else that's taking you away from culture), then when sales plateau, it can feel like something's wrong. How do you avoid that? How do you continue to add to the revenue component at the same time as creating a winning culture?

If you are now, like I was 20⁺ years ago, you may well be struggling with this idea, especially in your busy world. Let me say it can be too easy to over-complicate your business journey, after all, there are so many people all saying different things, offering advice and telling you what you should and shouldn't do. Simply do this; do what you feel is right, then make it better. **Have a compelling mission** you and your team believe in (culture) and your customers engage with, and work hard to make the world a better place. **Hire the right people**, not because you have to fulfil demand, but because you are planning to

Finally, **get some help**, the best help you can afford. The support and help I had in the early years gave me many 'lightbulb' moments, creating a winning culture was just one. What else is there you could be taking advantage of if only you knew.

See also
How To Get Recruitment Right First Time - Part 1 (p19)
How To Get Recruitment Right First Time - Part 2 (p25)
Make It Better Before Trying To Make It Bigger (p103)
How To Solve The Problem Of The Entrepreneurs Second See-Saw (p121)
How Do You Know If Those In Your Network Are The Right People? (p159)
What Makes A Great Footballer? (p173)

Mark Jarvis

What We Can Learn From Not-For-Profit Organisations

I'm privileged to have a business ownership journey over 30 years, across multiple businesses. Have I enjoyed the journey, for the most part yes! Of course, there have been many challenges along the way, some big, some small, but I've learned so much. It's one of those key lessons I would like to share with you now by answering this question:

WHAT CAN WE LEARN FROM NOT-FOR-PROFIT ORGANISATIONS?

I've worked with hundreds of organisations over the years and I asked myself why is it that some organisations can get tens or even hundreds of people to show up regularly, on time and with a positive mindset when they are not paid a wage, have any employee benefits, or any other form of compensation for turning up and giving their time?

ONE WORD CAME TO MIND - PURPOSE

Traditionally we have on one side, profit driven businesses, and on the other side we have not-for-profit businesses. We even call them not-for-profit. I'm including charities, social enterprises etc. Any organisation where to serve is the aim, not to build profits

So, if they are not-for-profit, what do they stand for? I think 'purpose' is the answer.

For years, profit and purpose have seen mutually exclusive. You can't have both. What I'm discovering, and I think this is what all thriving organisations are discovering too, is that purpose and profit fuel one another. The more purpose you have, the more profit you have, and the more profit you have, the more purpose you can have. I'm also finding that the younger demographic are saying, "What are you doing as a business and as a business leader to help the world improve? What are you doing beyond selling your products and services to grow socially, sustainably and ethically?" This is very encouraging to me as our world evolves where I'm seeing our younger generations really wanting to help the world become a better place, and they're looking to engage with businesses and organisations to do that.

Having a compelling purpose really helps your business. The most interesting thing about that is it's not just about attracting more customers. A recent GALLUP poll discovered that now employees and team members want to be part of an organisation with purpose at its heart. Of course, the monthly wage packet is important, but more and more want to know what purpose is waiting for them at the office when they get there

Not-for-profit, charities and social enterprises have always known that purpose drives their organisation. As business owners, this is a very profitable lesson to learn from them.

LET'S DIG A LITTLE DEEPER...

As a successful business owner, I know that when I compete on price, my margins are squeezed, and if I keep doing it, I will become less and less profitable

We have all at some point been attracted by a price matching offe , for some businesses, it's how they gain market share, but it's fundamentally flawed as it restricts the ability of a business to increase profits. I've written extensively about this approach elsewhere, so I'm not going to repeat myself, suffic to say - in our modern world, purpose wins every time and we are willing to pay a little more for a product or service if we love the company.

When you connect with and promote your purpose, what you're actually doing is connecting with the heart of your customer, and the heart of your customer is where buying decisions are made. When you win their heart, your greatest competitor can never beat you. You may be thinking this doesn't apply to me, but I have news for you - it does! Whether you are service or product based, B2B or B2C, **at the heart of every buying decision, at any level, is a human who makes decisions based on how they feel, and how they feel about you**.

So how does an organisation get tenss or hundreds of people to show up and give their time when they are only paid in coffee and cake? Answer - they have a compelling reason or purpose for doing so. When you can take your great product or service and combine it with a really compelling purpose, you can win the heart of your customer, and that's a game changer. That's a win win win.

HOW DOES A FOR PROFIT ORGANISATION FIND A PURPOSE?

Apart from a very few exceptions, most businesses are built around an idea that has to do with a product or a service, not a purpose. So, your business is up and running, you've already got a board of directors, you're already manufacturing something, selling a product or service, and now I'm saying you need to add purpose to it? The challenge lies in making this genuine, because it can feel like a gimmick to everyone both inside and outside the business.

**HOW DOES AN EXISTING BUSINESS
OR ORGANISATION FIND OR DISCOVER PURPOSE?**

This is an interesting question because most, if not every, business or organisation did start with a purpose. The reason the founder decided to start the business was not because they had a product or service they wanted to bring to market, but because they recognised a gap in the market their product or service could fill, and by extension, make the world a better place. As the business grows and scales, purpose very often gets lost, and it's purpose which makes a difference in the modern world

What I've realised over the last ten plus years as our world has evolved is, a business is no longer about what it tells customers in their marketing, advertising and sales messages, it is about what its customers tell other customers it is. This is where the game has changed. When you can create a compelling purpose and get other customers to talk about it, they will fuel your growth. When customers fuel your growth, sustainable and healthy growth is created and it increases loyalty in your teams.

WHEN WAS THE LAST TIME YOU PURCHASED SOMETHING WITHOUT READING A REVIEW?

Any business can tell me all day long how much better they are than their competitors and why their products are superior, but there's a lack of credibility because there's obvious bias, but when others say how great you are, that wins the day. There are so many online review platforms popping up for this very point.

We all know that positive word of mouth advertising is the most powerful form of advertising available to us, but because we don't know how to work that out, we usually end up spending all our time and energy, and sometimes money, on paid advertising, marketing and social media, where we only shout about ourselves, what we are doing and what we've done. Is it any wonder that more and more people are realising they are just adding to the noise because it's not building a sustainable solution to growth.

HOW DOES THIS CONNECT TO PURPOSE?

Simply this - word-of-mouth is really about sharing your purpose. It's so important you must read the other chapters on this topic. I have a full course on my website that shows you how to unlock and communicate your purpose as it applies to your marketing, sales, brand and team loyalty.

LET'S GET YOU STARTED ON THE RIGHT PATH

By asking these simple questions, you can start to remember, unlock or discover your purpose.

QUESTION ONE: WHAT DO YOU **WANT** TO BE KNOWN FOR?

Pretty straight forward question, but to answer it fully, it has to be answered in terms of how you are making the world a better place, not just why your products and services are bigger and better than others. Ask your team members what you are known for and if there's confusion in the office there will be confusion in the marketplace and amongst your prospects. Answering this question gets you on the path to clarifying your compelling purpose.

QUESTION TWO: WHAT **ARE** YOU KNOWN FOR?

The first question is all about clarifying your compelling purpose. This second question can be difficult many shy away from it because it feels too hard, or perhaps answering the question might reveal something you don't want to know.

This is what most people don't know - When what you want to be known for is what you ARE known for, your compelling purpose becomes your unique niche in the marketplace, and you create a sales force for free.

THERE IS NO PERFECT ORGANISATION

The reality of having the answer to these two questions expertly connected with no gaps is, of course, the aim, but does anyone actually get there. I suspect very few. What we can learn is the main goal of every business or organisational team should be to shrink the gap between these two questions, and we shouldn't be scared of that. We should embrace that fact that we are imperfect, and every day we get to work on closing that gap.

HOW DO YOU CLOSE THE GAP?

By changing your focus... Every business or organisation has a focus. For most it's firmly rooted in themselves, who are we, what are we doing, what we will do next. This forms the core of almost every form of advertising, marketing and internal goal setting, and we have already discussed why this is not sustainable in an increasingly noisy world. I've realised every business or organisation has to be and exist for more than just themselves. In our modern world, if your goal is just to stay in business and make money, then you probably won't. A sweeping and harsh statement you may think, so let's explore.

When the focus or spotlight of a business is on themselves, their purpose (back to that again) is never clear and they will most likely end up competing on a level they wish they could escape from (typically price as discussed).

When your focus is on your customer, you will ask them how you can serve them better, you will win their hearts, they will create positive word-of-mouth for you and become your sales force. This may sound a little too easy, it's not. However, it is simple and most give up on this modern reality because they don't know how.

When your focus is on your team and they share your compelling purpose, they will rally behind the organisation and its message, and they will prosper in their role.

When your focus is on your community, everyone around you (whether paid or unpaid) knows and understands the purpose and vision of the organisation and talks about it openly and proudly with others.

WHAT HAVE WE LEARNED?

First of all, when what you **WANT** to be known for is what you **ARE** known for, your compelling purpose becomes your unique niche in the marketplace, and you create a sales force for free.

Secondly, thriving organisations are more concerned with becoming fans of their customers, team and community instead of trying to get their customers to become fans of the business. When you compare this statement to a lot of the marketing and advertising out there, it's the opposite. It's all about them.

Customer, team and community engagement is about winning their hearts to your purpose by proactively engaging with them, putting the spotlight on them, and taking the spotlight off the organisation.

WHAT HAVE WE LEARNED FROM NOT-FOR-PROFIT ORGANISATIONS?

When you have a compelling purpose, you don't need flashy advertising to win the hearts of your customers. We've been spending money with charities for decades, with no hint of a product or service in return. It's simply because we believe in their purpose.

I'LL CLOSE WITH THIS SUGGESTION

Next time you're talking with your customers, your team, and in your community, ask them what they think your purpose is. Now all you have to do is close the gap...

See also
How To Avoid The Catch When Finding Your Purpose (p11)
How To Get Recruitment Right First Time - Part 1 (p19)
How To Get Recruitment Right First Time - Part 2 (p25)
Why Start-Ups Sometimes Fail (p57)
Make It Better Before Trying To Make It Bigger (p103)

Invest Quality In Your Quantity

Investing quality in your quantity will ensure your business is growing with an infinite mindset, always working towards better, and keeping you at the top of your game.

The performance and sustainability of any business depends on quality, whether it is in service or products, and quality is relevant to every aspect of your profession and business.

One final, and probably the most important point, quality begins with yourself.

If you as individuals, directors, partners, managers etc, are not working to better yourself and bring quality to everything you do, then you can never hope to achieve quantity.

How To Unlock The Power Of Focus

Before we get to unlocking the power of focus, I would like to begin by dispelling a couple of myths from my own experiences as a business owner. It took me a long time to work out how to harness the personal and organisational power of focus. I'm not sure exactly why it took me so long, perhaps part of it was I assumed two things about leadership that just aren't true. Perhaps it took me so long because I don't think anybody ever told me, or if they did, I was too self-absorbed to listen!

To begin with, I think I assumed that good leaders are good at everything. The good leaders I'd read about, listened to or watched, seemed to be good at everything they did. Everything around them went so well and looked, at least to my eyes, seamless and productive. I began to assume you just have to be good at everything. Whatever someone asks you to do, you have to be able to do, and have the answer.

It took me a while to realise that's not true. In fact, good leaders are rarely good at many things. They're generally good at one or two things. They have worked out how to focus on those one or two things and surround themselves with others who are good at their own, different one or two things.

The second myth is that I assumed was good leaders focused on their weaknesses in order to make them strengths. Traditionally, this is what the SWOT analysis tool has always taught us right? Why focus on a strength when you could focus on your weaknesses and turn them into strengths. The problem there is that your weaknesses are just that - something you're not good at.

That's how I started, trying to be good at everything. Now don't get me wrong, I know if you're just starting up, you do have to do a little bit of many different things, but as your business grows and scales, you need to adopt a different approach or you will just stay stuck following these two, and other business myths.

I started out coasting through things I was already good at, and I would just work hard at getting better at something I was never going to be good at, much less great at. My weaknesses got marginally better, while my strengths didn't get developed. So, four or five years into my journey, I finally discovered this massively important principle that "**My fully exploited strengths are of far greater value to my organisation than my marginally improved weaknesses**", because my weaknesses will only be marginally improved no matter how hard I work at them.

So once I got past the number one myth - I don't have to be great at everything, not even everything I'm responsible for; and number two - I need to focus on my strengths because my strengths are the value add to whatever it is that I know and decide to do professionally. So this at last got me in the game of learning to understand the power of focus.

The power of focus lies in only doing what only you can do (read that again….). In other words, if your fully exploited strengths are the greatest value add to the organisation, then the focus is to only do what only you can do. When I say 'only you can do', I don't mean there are other people who can't do it, but within your organisation, you are the best person to do it. You should focus on adding value where you add the most value and thais is going to be tied to your strengths.

I've already said that early on, you have to do a little bit of everything, it's both natural and necessary. It's natural, because early on you set the standards and it's necessary because sometimes there's nobody else to do it. What took me too long to work out was what may initially be natural and necessary, would ultimately limit my effect veness as a leader if I had stayed in those roles for too long, either because I was enjoying the drama, I couldn't let go, I wanted to micromanage or I just couldn't find anybody else to do it.

Stay in those roles too long and you risk dumbing down the whole organisation, and the IQ of the organisation never reaches maximum potential because again, you're not focused on the things where you add the most value.

The first power of focus lies in understanding that "The less you do, the more you accomplish". This power doesn't mean you do less work, but less different things - you are more focussed. Not intuitive I agree, which is why many get stuck and never break through to the next level of business ownership.

The second power of focus lies in understanding that "The less you do, the more you empower others to accomplish". The basic premise of leadership and organisational intelligence.

PUTTING IT ALL TOGETHER (AND COSTS)

What this means for you is that the less (differe t) things you do, the more you accomplish because when you're working in your strengths zone, you accomplish more.

The less (different) things you do means that you will create space for other people to do what they do best. These two points are far more than just nice to have. I would go as far to say they are mission critical for any organisation because there's actually a cost to pay organisationally if you don't get these right.

When an organisational leader or somebody within the organisation doesn't understand principle number one, their perceived value to the organisation is diminished. The reason their perceived value is diminished is because they're not doing what brings the most value to the organisation - they are not working in their strengths zone. The second thing which happens if you don't get this right, is the perceived value of other leaders in the organisation is diminished because they don't get an opportunity to do what they do best.

And thirdly, the ability of the organisation to keep great leaders is diminished because people won't stay where they're not able to thrive. When they're not able to lead, manage or work in an area where they feel they are thriving based on their skill set, they will start to wonder whether an opportunity to work somewhere where they can spend most of their time doing what they do best, and where they can add the most value, becomes a lot more attractive. I hope you can see, this isn't just an add on, this really is mission critical for organisations that want to thrive.

WHAT'S THE GOAL

The goal is to build a well-rounded and intelligent organisation by focussing on people's strengths, including your own, and not to become a 'well-rounded' leader who is great at couple of things and marginally good enough at other things. While you think you have to be great at everything, you are never going to be great at anything because you are not focussed. Again, **one of those key secrets it took me too long to learn.**

LET'S DIG A LITTLE DEEPER

Every leader, at some point, has authority over areas within their organisation in which they personally have little or possibly no expertise. This means they are responsible for getting things done they don't know how to do. When a leader can't distinguish between their authority and their core strengths, they often find themselves making decisions in areas where they don't have expertise. Which, in turn, undermines the decisions of other people. It effects efficien , it effects morale, and it effects the value of your team and yourself, and things get worse, they don't get better.

So the tip here is **leverage your authority as little as possible, and leverage your strengths as much as possible**. This will help you unlock the power of focus.

THE NEXT POINT I WANT TO MAKE IS ABOUT SELF-AWARENESS

In many organisations ,as they grow and scale, the owner/leader is not aware of what they are best placed to do, they don't know their strengths. As discussed already, they may have done a SWOT analysis, found their weaknesses and tried to fix them, but have missed that success comes by leveraging their strengths. It could be that leaders are forced into roles and tasks because they have always done them, assumed they are good at them but missed that delegation could unlock growth in yourself and others, and increase the overall IQ of the organisation.

LACK OF SELF-AWARENESS IS A PROBLEM

For all the leaders out there, let me take some pressure off - it's okay not to be good at something. It's not okay to keep doing something you're not good at. I'll say that again because it's important! It's okay not to be good at things. It's not okay to keep doing the things you're not good at. Admitting a weakness does not diminish your effectiveness. Refusing to admit a weakness diminishes your effecti eness. When you acknowledge a weakness to others and seek help, it's never new information for the people you work with. They already know your weaknesses. Nobody is going to be surprised, they're actually relieved when you acknowledge what you don't know.

You feel guilty delegating things you don't enjoy because you assume nobody else will enjoy it either. Just because you hate doing something, doesn't mean everybody hates doing it too. I hate admin, I'm not good at it but my Executive Assistant (EA) loves it. I hate accounts but my accountant loves it. I hate marketing but my marketing department loves it, same for my sales department - I think you get the idea. So, in your effort to be a good example, you do things that you know and let other people do what they enjoy. My weakness is somebody else's opportunity to shine. Keeping this in mind keeps us from falling into the trap of losing focus.

TAKE TIME TO DEVELOP OTHER LEADERS

The power of focus lies in taking the time to develop other leaders. Typically, in a growing organisation, no one has time to stop doing what needs to get done, to teach somebody to do what you're already doing. This becomes a problem, because you stay in roles you shouldn't stay in, and it becomes a barrier to the development of others because they don't get the opportunity to thrive in their strengths.

At some point, if you are committed to growth and progress, you have to get up out of those chairs and teach somebody else to sit there. Of course, there's some truth to the adage if you want something done right, do it yourself, but this again, becomes a barrier to your leadership and to the health of your organisation.

Leadership is not primarily about getting things done right. **Leadership is really about getting things done right through other people.** It's about multiplying your efforts through others, not using others, but empowering other people by positioning them to do what they do best. No doubt it is time consuming and inefficien to start with but the pay-off is massive

By working to your strengths, you can unlock the power of focus, and your organisation will become more intelligent, more productive and more profitable.

To sum up; we said earlier that **your fully exploited strengths are of far greater value to your organisation than your marginally improved weaknesses**. So focus on strengthening your strengths and look for ways to delegate your weaknesses.

Remember, asking for help is not a weakness, it's your way of delegating what you are not good at, to someone who is.

See also
How To Avoid Random Acts Of Delegation (p45)
The Key To Organisational Health (p93)
Why People Leave People (p111)
The 60:20:20 Rule (From The Jarvis Principles) (p197)
Five Top Tips For Managing A Growing Team (p229)

Mark Jarvis

The Key To Organisational Health

What makes a healthy organisation? Many people talk about organisational health in terms of pivoting, agility and effective planning and whilst these are all valid topics to cover, let's focus on what really makes a difference

In this book, I've already talked about making your organisation, 'Better before bigger', and I've also talked about 'How to get recruitment right first time'. Getting ahead of your competition is so much more than trying to second guess the future, or how the next alleged recession will impact your organisation. Why alleged recession? Some of the most successful global organisations were founded in recession, and those willing to find excuses for their lack of progress will always find something else to blame.

A HEALTHY ORGANISATION EQUALS A PROFITABLE ORGANISATION

Some think organisational intelligence is what's important, like gaining new knowledge and being smart. We are taught smart organisations succeed, and doing smart things like implementing a new strategy will bring the success you want.

No matter how much harder you stamp on the accelerator, if your car engine has a misfire, there's no way you're going to go any faster, or get any further!

Some think it's about marketing and technology, and lots of other things which are all really important and interesting of course, but real competitive advantage in a world where everybody has access to the same knowledge and information, is directly linked to the health of your organisation.

In our modern world, everybody has access to the same knowledge and information required to succeed, yet so many organisations are unhealthy. They're dysfunctional. There's politics, there's confusion, there's infighting, and there's turnover among good people who don't want to be there anymore. So more knowledge and information, more courses and workshops cannot be the only answer. Overcoming these challenges is the real competitive advantage. Remember to read - Better before bigger (page 103).

The healthiest organisations are the most resilient, **let's get into what you can do about it.**

MAKE YOUR LEADERSHIP TEAM MORE COHESIVE.

A cohesive leadership team is one that is aligned. It doesn't mean they agree on everything. In fact, they have to learn how to disagree constructively. This happens when there's trust, openness and vulnerability. I'm not talking about trust in terms of, 'I've known you for years so I can predict your behaviour and I can predict what you will do' type trust, and I'm not talking about vulnerability in terms of, 'someone has a secret over you that no one else knows'. But trust that says, 'I'm humble enough and vulnerable enough to admit when I'm wrong, to acknowledge when I don't know something, to admit when I make a mistake, or to even apologise or celebrate when your ideas are better than mine'. When people can be emotionally open and vulnerable, this kind of trust creates the foundation for every cohesive team and the whole organisation. Without this vulnerability, deep trust isn't going to be there.

WHEN THERE'S TRUST, THERE'S CONFLICT

What? Really? Yes, and here's why. Most people don't mind if their idea isn't taken forward as long as they feel heard. As long as everyone gets to be heard, even if they have conflicting ideas, you can build a healthy team. There's nothing worse than everyone agreeing to the loudest person's ideas in a meeting if they then go on to talk about not being listened to with their colleagues - a major reason why good people leave. Productive conflict means everyone has the opportunity to offer their ideas and perspectives, and the decision making moves the organisation forward.

CREATE ORGANISATIONAL CLARITY

Next to the first point where we began to make people behaviourally cohesive, now we are focussing on gaining clarity in the organisation. Some talk about Vision, Values and Mission, all good points to cover, but what does that mean if those in the organisation don't have clarity of purpose. How do you create organisational clarity whilst building your cohesive leadership team? When you have agreement around the answers to these six simple questions, you will have organisational clarity.

WHY DOES YOUR ORGANISATION EXIST?

What injustice are you trying to fix. It's not to make money or provide jobs or products and services, but because what you do makes a difference in the world

HOW DO YOU BEHAVE?

Again, this is not about Vision, Mission and Values because it's easy to come up with a list of values no one can remember. This is about intolerance. What behaviours will you be intolerant of before taking action. If you have an organisation without core behaviours, you don't know who to attract, and you don't know who to repel. Every organisation should repel the wrong people and attract the right people. Here's six example behaviours I and my teams live by: Make it better, Take it personally, Collaborate, Remain open minded, Replace yourself, Stay fit

WHAT DO YOU DO?

For most this is pretty easy, yet you may be surprised to learn that not everyone in the organisation can deliver the same message. Remember, this is about clarity throughout the organisation, not just getting it right. Do you sell products, do you provide services, are you a training and education business? How will your customers know what you do if you don't.

This becomes an even more interesting question when you think about how your team members talk to their friends outside work. Are they proud of what they do and who they serve?

HOW WILL YOU SUCCEED?

I'm asking these questions like this because 'why you exist' and 'how you behave' always come first in healthy, productive and profitable organisations. This goes far beyond the latest strategy or marketing plan. This is about how you implement success and how the way you succeed will give you a competitive edge. This is best defined using verbs and nouns, for example: Be better, Inspire our customers, Empower our people.

WHAT'S YOUR BIGGEST CURRENT PRIORITY?

This is a question that sits at the top of every meeting agenda. It gives a real sense of purpose and momentum to your team meetings because everyone knows what's happening in the organisation right now, and the meeting focus can be on what every person and every department can contribute towards the current organisational priorities. It also further strengthens the clarity we mentioned earlier.

Organisations in crisis are usually very good at focussing on a single priority and developing a plan to recover. What we are talking about here is not waiting for a crisis to focus, but gaining a competitive edge with a single, organisation-wide, priority to support growth.

Individuals and departments may have different tasks, but the message here is that everyone is pulling in the same direction.

WHO MUST DO WHAT?

Now your teams are behaviourally cohesive, you have clarity of purpose and you know what your top priorities are, you can start to think about who's best at coming up with the idea, evaluating the plan, getting people rallied around, and pushing it through to the end. Regardless of their job title, you can organise who does what, what needs to get done, and who's best to do it.

CONSTANT COMMUNICATION.

Most people understand the importance of a clear marketing message, but so many miss the importance of clear and constant communication (the clarity), of their purpose, behaviours and priorities throughout the whole organisation from CEO to the newest team member. Once you do the first two above, you've gained a competitive edge that most others will never achieve because they are still chasing the latest strategy and plan.

Gain clarity on the six questions I shared in above and talk about them all the time because they form the core of your organisation.

Have the courage not to think that the success of your organisation is based on your intelligence or the tactical decisions you make, but it's based on your character and your ability to build a healthy organisation through day-to-day and simple disciplines.

You don't have to be the smartest person in the room, but **you do have to have the security and vulnerability to surround yourself with people who are smarter than you, to keep it clear and simple, and the integrity to keep it whole.**

See also
How To Get Recruitment Right First Time - Part 1 (p19)
How To Get Recruitment Right First Time - Part 2 (p25)
How To Avoid Random Acts Of Delegation (p45)
The Secret To Cultural Success In Business (p71)
What Can We Learn From Non-Profit Organisations (p77)
How To Unlock The Power Of Focus (p85)
Make It Better Before Trying To Make It Bigger (p103)

The Five Things To Do When Creating A Team Skills Development Plan

Prioritising continuous learning and development both for yourself and for your team is more important than ever. To the point where more and more candidates are asking at interview; What will my career development plan look like? **As well as making your business more attractive to recruits, personal and professional development is a cornerstone in helping you remain competitive**. A well-designed plan not only enhances individual growth but also nurtures a culture of collaboration and innovation within the team. In this chapter, I'll explore the five most impactful areas to consider when creating a team skills development (or training) plan.

FIND OUT WHERE YOU ARE AND IDENTIFY GAPS

Obvious I'm sure but just so we know where we're starting; it's crucial to assess the existing skill sets within your team. You may already have an idea of these but it's well worth getting it all written down as a start point for each of your team, **don't forget to include yourself and your management and leadership team too**! Why? You are building future managers and leaders so a combined plan helps those who you may want to bring forward, to see what their pathway could look like.

Finding the gaps will help you identify strengths and weaknesses, as well as pinpoint the skills that require improvement. By understanding the current skills landscape, you can create targeted development plans which address the most critical gaps.

SET DEVELOPMENT GOALS THAT MATCH YOUR BUSINESS AND MISSION OBJECTIVES

To make your plan truly impactful, engaging and inspiring, align it with your organisation's broader business objectives and mission. Identify the key skills and competencies which are most relevant to achieving your strategic goals. For instance, if your company aims to expand into new markets, prioritise language skills, cross-cultural communication and understand the language of your new market. Aligning development goals with business objectives means the skills your team are acquiring directly contribute to organisational growth.

INVOLVE TEAM MEMBERS IN THE PLANNING PROCESS

Inclusion and participation are key. Involving team members in the planning process will encourage their active engagement and ownership. Conduct individual meetings or group discussions to understand their aspirations, career goals, and areas where they feel they need support and improvement. This is as much about what inclusivity brings over and above the individual's development journey and additional skills learned. Inclusivity brings a sense of ownership and commitment towards their professional development.

MAKE IT A TEAM PLAN WITH INDIVIDUAL MILESTONES

One size does not fit all when it comes to skills development. Recognise that each team member has unique strengths and ever-changing areas for improvement. Design tailored learning opportunities that address individual needs, learning styles and DISC* behaviours. Cater to people's diverse learning styles through internal workshops, external training programmes, mentorship initiatives, online courses and self-learning etc. Diverse learning activities means you will empower your team members to grow at their own pace and in ways that resonate with their learning style.

PROVIDE ONGOING SUPPORT, EVALUATION AND FEEDBACK

Creating a team skills development plan is not a one-time activity. It requires continuous support and evaluation to ensure its effectiveness. The framework I use with my clients includes a business plan, marketing plan, sales plan, recruitment plan, training plan, leadership and management plan, and finance plan, all integrated together.

Offer ongoing support to your team members by providing resources, feedback, and coaching throughout their development journey. Regularly review and assess progress against the set goals and support them to make their own adjustments as needed. Encourage a culture of continuous learning and provide opportunities for sharing knowledge and best practices within the team.

*DISC is a behavioural assessment and profiling tool I've found essential in aligning my team members. I also use it during the recruitment process.

See also
How To Get Recruitment Right First Time - Part 1 (p19)
How To Get Recruitment Right First Time - Part 2 (p25)
How To Avoid Random Acts Of Delegation (p45)
The Secret To Cultural Success In Business (p71)
What Can We Learn From Not-For-Profit Organisations (p77)
The Key To Organisational Health (p93)

What Is Momentum In Business

After a 'body' or business has started it needs something to keep it developing or progressing. This is momentum.

WHAT IS MOMENTUM IN BUSINESS?

Simply the ability to maintain traction, overcome friction, and maintain pace on the journey that is business.

Here are three things to help you gain and maintain momentum in your business and get things done:

1. Understand what works and what doesn't in the real world.
2. Know how to implement what works.
3. Commit to action and investment.

Here are some additional questions to ask yourself - be honest!

Do you have a vision for your business, or has it got lost because you are busy?

Do you know what to do, how to do it, and where you are going, or are you just working in the here and now?

Are you working towards growth and better outcomes or are you settled on just doing more?

There is no doubt in my mind that success comes from the momentum you build on your business journey. Where is your journey leading you?

Make it Better Before Trying to Make it Bigger

I am often asked to sit in on management meetings and recently I was reminded of a quote from one of the board members of a large fried chicken company (no names). Before I get to that, let me give you a little context.

The meeting I attended was my client's regular monthly review and planning session, though this time with more of a focus into next year. As usual, we reviewed performance against goals and talked about what needs to change to reach the next set of goals. As well as talking about influ ncing economic factors, we also talked about a rising level of competition - they felt one particular competitor was gaining traction in their market and was becoming a threat. Unsurprisingly, this sparked a vibrant discussion on setting bigger goals, how to grow bigger, how to grow faster, how to do more marketing, and how to win against their competition.

If you've been following me for a while, you will already know my thoughts on just doing more and expecting different results

Just to be clear, my role in these meetings is to listen in, evaluate progress, offer thoughts and suggestions when asked, and a perspective when needed.

Having listened to the bigger, faster, more, bigger, faster, more discussion for several minutes, I suggested a different wa , a way that makes things better.

Consider this concept, *"If you get better, your customers will demand that you get bigger."* Rather than try to do more, faster, let's do better. When we do better and your competition is just doing more, you will always outperform them.

Now, with this idea, they were able to start thinking differentl , better in fact.

Here are some of the key points they are now implementing that you can take away to help you make it better too.

Firstly, if you are going to make anything better, you have to decide what better looks like and what it means. **You have to seek clarification**.

In the lifecycle of a business or organisation, it's tempting to take your foot off the throttle once you reach a level of success you are happy with - the problem with this philosophy is that others will make it better if you do not, and they will overtake you.

When faced with failure in an organisation, we are always drawn to find out what went wrong and why it didn't work. Very rarely do we apply the same principle to success - why did it work and how can we make it better - because the assumption is that if nothing is wrong then nothing needs fixing and therefore nothing can be bette .

As a quick aside - this is often the point that your team member starts thinking they can do it better than you, they leave your business to join another, or setup on their own.

CLARIFY THE **WIN**

What's the win for every critical point in your business, from sales and marketing to admin and growth, clarify the win in such a way that everybody understands what you're trying to do. Setting goals has an outcome, it's something you can reach. But **you can experience a win because it creates a journey which engages people**.

Clarifying the win takes time. I think leaders often think they don't have time for this. They think, 'Let's just know what we're doing, we're selling stuff, we're building stuff, we're hiring people, we're looking for a new market etc'. Stopping long enough to clarify the win and creating terminology everybody can embrace is huge, but it takes time.

When you can articulate the win, not just the goal, there's more energy, it's easier to communicate and I think it's easier for your team to rally around. So if you're going to make anything better, you've got to know what the win is and what better looks and feels like.

We all make discissions based on emotions and then justify our discissions with facts. Clarifying the win for a client is not about the product or service, it's about how they feel about working with you and how their sense of fulfilment has increased. How owning your product make your clients feel, and that feeling is the win.

What's the win for your team? I hope you're not thinking it's the pay-check or benefits package you offe , because it's not. The win for your team lies in job satisfaction and fulfilm nt. I will go to work because I want to and if you think it's because I have to, I won't be with you very much longer. Clarify your wins across every aspect of your organisation in terms of how it makes people feel, only then can you focus on making it better and therefore bigger.

ONCE YOU HAVE CLARIFICATION, YOU CAN EVALUATE

Everybody has some kind of evaluation and feedback process in their organisation, but evaluation on its own is no better than the standard against which you're evaluating. It goes back to the point about clarity - what are you trying to do, and what's the win and what could make it better.

The theme of this chapter is 'How do you make it better?', and you can't make it better if all you do in your evaluation sessions is to try and fix what's broken. You have to evaluate what worked in order to make it better. So again, the way you conduct your evaluations determines whether or not evaluation really is a leverage point for making your organisation better.

Remember, **getting things right is not the goal, making things better is**.

When you're confronted with failure, it's natural to ask why disaster struck. Unfortunately, success doesn't trigger such soul searching. Success is commonly interpreted as evidence not only that your existing strategy and practices work, but also that you have all the knowledge and information you need. So **sometimes success is the worst enemy of making anything better**. If you want to make things better, then you must evaluate success as well as failure and this is not intuitive for most leaders. Perhaps part of the reason why, is that you are always in a hurry, believing that more, bigger and faster are the answers to success when in fact **growth comes only from doing better**.

Fresh eyes and ears will always offer a perspective you may not currently have, as it did with my client in their meeting, because, if you stare at something long enough it will disappear in plain sight.

Remember, good is not good enough. Anything worth doing, is worth doing better.

See also
How To Avoid Random Acts Of Delegation (p45)
Why People Leave People (p111)
What Are Big Goals And What Are Ordinary Goals? (p129)
What Makes A Great Footballer? (p173)

Be, Do, Have - What Does it Mean?

Yesterday in a conversation I was reminded about the BE - DO - HAVE concept, and how so many seem to get this concept mixed up.

First, let's explore what BE - DO - HAVE means.

Put as simply as possible, **this concept is all about BEING the person you want to be and DOING the right things in order to HAVE the life and experiences you want.**

I have found this is very different to what many people actually do.

Like many concepts in our world, we talk about being, doing and having in that order, yet what I often see is people focusing on having, doing and then being.

Many focus on what they want to HAVE in life, having goals and having a plan in order to get them to a destination and some measure of their success.

They then use a plan to write down what they need to DO in order to HAVE what they want without first understanding they need to BE in the right mindset in order to DO the right things, so they can HAVE the life and experiences and world they want.

For example, **this is how many who ask for my help start out...**

"If only I could HAVE (more time, more customers, more profit, a more loyal team), I could DO what I want to do, and then I could BE happy...".

The biggest problem? If, could, and try are speculative and may never come, Yet you can choose who you want to BE today!

If you are going to see success, whatever success might mean for you, first, decide who you are going to BE, what you stand for and what you believe in.

Then everything you DO will be aligned to who you are, which means that everything you HAVE now and will HAVE in the future is based on you BEING the best version of yourself.

Next time you are thinking about setting quantity-based goals and plans. take a moment to think about the order you plan in. First think about who you want to BE because BEING the person you want to be means that you can DO **the things necessary to HAVE the things you want. Not the other way around**.

See also
How To Unlock The Power Of Focus (p85)
What Are Big Goals And What Are Ordinary Goals? (p129)
Possibilities And Probabilities (p133)

Why Do Drama When Drama-free Is A Choice?

Have you heard of the Triple Filter Test? If not, here it is ...

Most often attributed to Socrates (pronounced Sock-rat-ees, not So-Crates as in the Bill and Ted movie), this is a way of testing which information is True, Good and Useful.

My take on this approach is what I use to decide on how I live my life and who and what information I engage with.

The premise is: imagine you have the opportunity to receive a piece of information.

Before you read, listen or watch it, ask these three questions.

1. Does the person or source of the information know for sure that it is true? If the answer is no, I choose not to engage. This is the main reason I don't listen to media broadcasts and hearsay. 'Today's truth is tomorrow's lies'.
2. Is the information kind and good? Is it kind to me, kind to the person giving it and kind to the person it's about? If the answer is no, I choose not to engage.
3. Is the information useful? Does it help me, does it help the person giving it and does it help the person it's about? If the answer is no, I choose not to engage.

What can we learn from this concept for our business?

Is the person you are connecting with or buying from, genuinely out to support your aims and help you, or are they just out to help themselves? Are you doing the same?

There are more than enough good and kind people out there who have true and useful things to say. Why choose negativity, frustration, misdirection and drama when you can make a choice?

What have you heard, seen or listened to today that did not pass the Triple Filter Test?

I would be very surprised if it's not at least one thing.

See also
Be, Do, Have - What does it mean? (p107)
Make it better before trying to make it bigger (p103)
How do you know if those in your network are the right people? (p159)
What does making changes in business really mean? (p163)
Which question I am asked most often (p209)

Why People Leave People

People don't leave bad jobs, they leave bad bosses.

It's long been known that people don't leave businesses, they leave people, and they often leave because of a breakdown in communication and in the relationships between colleagues, managers and leaders.

Only now, as we are beginning to return to the workplace following forced work from home policies (post the Covid-19 pandemic), are we finding out the true cost of the breakdown in communication. **More people than ever decided it was time to change job or role, or even start up their own business.**

The problem is our managers and leaders were not equipped to recognise their responsibility to increase their communication skills, all the while trying to cope with their own situation, keep working, and keep their team productive.

The story is the same to a great to lesser extent, across every industry; just maintaining the level of service their customers expect is challenging because they are a team member down, their recruitment pool is too thin, or they just can't recruit quickly enough.

In the same way as retaining a customer is easier and cheaper than gaining a new customer, the simplest answer seems to be **get better at retaining your existing team.**

Easier said than done I hear you say, and you are right. Most seem to think increasing a salary offer and adding more benefits to employment is enough. Sadly, most are finding out that whilst it may encourage short-term loyalty, employers are not addressing the fundamental reason the team member considered resigning in the first place - it was because of the people.

Research carried out in March 2022 by Wiley & Sons indicated the number one reason people consider leaving is because **they don't feel valued or recognised by their line manager** for their contribution to the team. The research also suggests that whilst many managers and leaders recognise they need to upskill, most simply don't know where to start, or have the time and resources to do so.

PEOPLE DON'T LEAVE THE BUSINESS, THEY LEAVE THE PEOPLE

As a manager or leader in your organisation you are always encouraging your team to develop themselves, you probably provide some level of training and personal development programmes, yet are you doing the same for yourself, or are you just too busy?

WHY ELSE DO PEOPLE LEAVE?

Based on conversations I've had in businesses and organisations, it can be because the team member has received so much support and training, they feel they have overtaken their manager, and now feel confident to strike out on their own. This is not to say you shouldn't upskill your team just to keep them, of course not - but you must upskill yourself to continually inspire others to greater success.

Learning how to create an environment of clear, inclusive and collaborative communication is a key step in increasing long term loyalty in your team, and it starts with you.

Remember - **team members typically start thinking about leaving 3 months before you know anything about it.** Unless you learn how to mitigate this process, you will always be this busy looking for your next hire, either to expand or just to stay afloat

WHERE TO START:

Start with something simple that makes a big and positive impact on productivity and really helps people feel included.

I've been using DISC to aid communication, team and culture building in organisations for years and it really does make a difference quickly. If you've never heard of DISC before, basically it's a powerful life tool that helps you navigate relationships so **you are better equipped to boost productivity and positively influence loyalty.** It also aids engagement and alignment in the recruiting process too.

HOW'S THE TEAM DYNAMIC IN YOUR BUSINESS?

Could there be something simmering you don't know about?

A good clue is how many times you have to ask someone to complete or follow up on a task.

Focusing on becoming a productive manager and inspiring leader will increase loyalty in your organisation and help you to stop worrying about team retention and recruitment.

See also
How To Get Recruitment Right First Time - Part 1 (p19)
How To Get Recruitment Right First Time - Part 2 (p25)
How To Avoid Random Acts Of Delegation (p45)
What We Can Learn From Not-For-Profit Organisations (p77)
Make It Better Before Trying To Make It Bigger (p103)

Why Referrals Can Be Hard Work

Imagine this, you visit your local GP and talk through your symptoms. Having talked, your GP decides that you are best referred to a specialist.

You may have spent a fair amount of time with your GP so when you arrive, the specialist has the majority of information they need from your GP to be able to solve your problem.

Imagine if your GP referred you to a specialist and you had the same conversation all over again, time consuming and unnecessary right?

Let's transfer this into the business world and imagine that the GP is someone who refers you regularly and the specialist is a prospect of yours that you are being referred to.

I believe that referrals can be hard work because you are not training your referrers (GP's) well enough. A real referral means you have been 'pre-sold', ie. The prospect (specialist) knows why you are there, and what problem you will solve for them, without you having to explain it all over again.

For me, the essence of true relationship (referral) marketing is the ability of your network to refer you simply, clearly and to your ideal prospect rather than the random, accidental and often time-consuming recommendations you currently receive.

What is the most frustrating aspect of the 'referrals' you receive?

What Are The Four Things On The Mind Of Every Business Owner?

No matter what you do and no matter what the latest technological trend, there are four key questions on the mind of every business owner.

1. Time - how can I find time to do all the things I need to do?
2. Team - how can I build my team so they are as driven as I am?
3. Money - how can I manage my cash-flow so my business is increasingly profitable

I believe discovering what to do to answer those three questions is simply a few taps on the keyboard away in a world where we all have access to the same information anytime we want it, the answers are freely available and accessible to all of us equally.

For example - I have just asked a well-known AI platform this question - 'How can I find the time to do all the things I need to do in business?' Guess what, in just a few seconds, it gave me 10 tips and ideas about what I could do. Message me if you want them or try it yourself.

NOW I KNOW WHAT TO DO, ALL I NEED TO DO IS DO IT RIGHT?

Here's where most come unstuck - they believe the solution lies in knowing what to do. Trust me when I say that solutions lie in implementing knowledge, not just knowing it. Even though I asked the AI 'How can I….' it still came back with what to do. Applying knowledge is still requires a human.

This brings me on to the 4th and most important question - *'How am I going to implement this new learning in my business?'*

TO ANSWER THAT QUESTION, A RADICAL RE-THINK IS NECESSARY.

In our modern world, no one can sell knowledge for money because it's free to all. Knowledge is no longer power, the power lies in implementation, and implementation can only be delivered by a human, whether by you because you have levelled-up your mindset, or because you have asked for help from someone who already knows HOW to use that knowledge and information.

The search engines revolutionised our ability to access information and knowledge, now AI is doing the same in terms of accessibility, I won't say value, you can decide that.

Who knows whether implementation will be available to anyone anytime in the future in the same way as knowledge is now. For now, the ability to implement knowledge comes from experience. **I believe many of the challenges we face as business owners can be solved if we simply decide to take action and get help from those who know HOW.**

See also
How to leverage AI in business (p35)
Why creative distraction is holding you back (p65)
Why are my clients not held accountable? (p153)
What does making changes in business really mean? (p163)
Which question I am asked most often (p209)

Is Today Your Last Groundhog Day?

Have you ever had one of those days when you have that feeling of déjà vu, you feel like you've been here before? I think we all feel like that from time to time....

This got me thinking about the 1993 movie *Groundhog Day* where the main character gets stuck reliving the same day over and over again until he gets a revelation about how to take his life forward. In this case, because it's a romantic comedy style movie, it's about the hero discovering he needs the heroine and they all live happily ever after... Sorry to spoil the plot but it is a great movie to watch with your partner on a rainy afternoon.

If you've seen the movie, I hope you can connect with the plot lines as I show you how they relate to the life many of us experience today. If you haven't seen the movie, put it on your weekend watch list, then come back and re-read these messages.

The movie starts with Phil, the hero played by Bill Murray, having a job he doesn't enjoy and a life he doesn't love, waking up one morning to the same song on the radio. As he begins his day, he finds himself having the same conversations with the same people as he did yesterday. He repeats the same actions with the same outcomes and, as this continues day after day, **he becomes increasingly despondent.**

Over time, Phil begins to realise he has feelings for Rita, the heroine played by Andie MacDowell, he tries to learn about her passions and hobbies and get to know her, knowing that he can start again tomorrow if his attempts at befriending her don't work.

Unsurprisingly, all his attempts fail until his revelation. He discovers that being himself works when artificially creating situations does not. **So our hero embarks on a journey of learning and self-development to better himself** and become the person he is proud to be with a life he loves. And guess what… he gets the girl as all good romantic heroes do.

WHAT CAN WE LEARN FROM THIS STORY?

As a mentor and business coach **I see too many businesspeople stuck in a life they don't love because what they wanted at that beginning still eludes them.** It's true they may be ok, they are probably busy and busy means successful right?

Wrong…. why? Because their dreams and ambitions move increasingly further away. Most keep repeating the same old tasks, doing more of the same old work hoping that the harder they work and the more things they try, the closer they will get to their desired outcomes.

If we learned anything from Phil and his revelation, it is that **trying more and more, harder and harder to artificially influence your outcome does not work, in reality as much as in fiction.**

For you to get what you want, you need to change. Not work hard to change the things around you, what you do and how you do it, but change the way you think, as Phil, our hero did.

Scaling a business requires that people change because when people change, those people can change things - not the other way around.

See also
How To Unlock The Power Of Focus (p85)
Make It Better Before Trying To Make It Bigger (p103)
Be, Do, Have - What Does It Mean? (p107)

Mark Jarvis

How To Solve The Problem Of The Entrepreneurs Second See-Saw

I believe the 'second see-saw' is just one of many challenges that face businesses owners as they grow and develop their business.

As someone who regularly works with businesses facing this and many other challenges, I believe this solution to the second see-saw challenge will be useful for you too.

FIRSTLY, LET'S CLARIFY WHAT THE FIRST SEE-SAW CHALLENGE LOOKS LIKE

Imagine this, (you may even be here yourself).

You've started your business, it's doing well, and you now find yourself investing your time in marketing, which draws you into getting new business then delivering the business, getting the next piece of business, then delivering, then getting, then delivering, then getting, then delivering, see-sawing between getting and delivering.

THE FIRST SEE-SAW IS TIME, THE SECOND SEE-SAW IS PROFITABILITY.

Imagine this, (you may even be here yourself).

You've grown your business to the point where you need to expand, for many, this looks like employing your next team member. Before this happens, you may have already outsourced your accounts, social media and admin and now you need more capacity to grow.

The second see-saw is 'I need to take on someone, but I can't afford to until I get more business, but I can't get more business until I employ someone'.

Just do it I hear you say, and you'd be right. What takes a hit with this strategy? Profits

You have, from day 1 in your expansion, to pay another salary and it will take time for your turnover to build to match and cover that investment, typically up to 3 months. What if there were another way, a better way?

A BETTER WAY

Imagine this, (if you are here already, you're amazing, you've learned a better way).

You gain a new client, that client refers you to a second, the second client refers you to a third, the third to a fourth, then the first refers you again, the fourth to a fifth, the second again, the fifth to a sixth - I think you get the idea...

The key here; does this happen consistently, giving you a predictable flow of referrals?

Based on a very simple model, we have now smoothed the motion of the first and second see-sa .

- Because it takes 6-8 hours to gain a new client but just 10mins to get a referral, saving you huge amounts of time.
- Because you can spend much more time delivering, you are far more profitable, which means that growing your team has less impact on profits

HOW DO YOU GET STARTED?

The most obvious answer is to just ask for referrals, and whilst this will help, it's proven not to create a predictable flow of repeat referrals. Before you ask, in my experience, financial (or other) incentives do not work in the long term.

For me, my clients and those around me the answer is simple; **build relationships with a network of Referral Partners who refer you often, to your ideal target market** - you can use some of the time you save chasing new clients and invest it in your relationships.

As well as building your own network of referrals partners, there are a number of peer-to-peer referral based professional networking groups, definitely worth checking them out to kick-start your referrals strategy.

See also
The Reality Of Referrals In Business (p135)
Why Aren't You More Profitable In Your Network? (p149)
How To Plan For Increased Productivity Through Professional Networking (p155)
How Do You Know If Those In Your Network Are The Right People? (p159)
Which Came First, The Sale Pipeline Or The Relationship Pipeline? (p167)
The Top Seven Barriers To Consistent Quality Referrals (p203)
Time Limited Turnover - The Eternal Business Challenge (p225)
Are You Working In Transaction World Or Relationship World (p235)

How To Stop Worrying About Getting More Business

Stop worrying about where your next customer will come from and how to get more business because more of what you are already getting is easy.

Here is a story of a client and their worries.

On a lovely, sunny and fresh afternoon, I met with a business owner who told me all about their business and what they do. They have seen some amazing growth and successes over the years and are very positive about the future. I asked them if they were busy and of course the answer was yes - who isn't busy right?

So I asked them what their business will look like this time next year. Their answer - "We'll be busier, we'll have a bigger team and we'll be making more money." - Pretty standard answers. I went on to ask them:

- "How can you be busier if you are already busy?"
- "How can you have bigger team if you can't fund the salaries?"
- "How can you make more money if you are only funding more people to be busier?"

These were less easy to answer and perhaps for you too.

I believe the answer is to attract better business because it's easy to attract more of what you are already getting. Better business is smarter business and smarter business requires smarter people. Learn something new that your future-self will thank you for and work hard on smart things.

What's Your Inner Geek?*

We all have an inner geek somewhere within us. Sometimes it's linked to one of our passions in life and sometimes it's a general interest. What's your inner geek?

One of my inner geeks is of course people growth and scaling businesses. As well as a foodie geek and a petrolhead geek, I have a further science geek within me, and it is this one I am going to unleash on you today.

I'm going to lay some science on you (don't worry, I'm not going all Brian Cox), and I am going to show you how this aspect of science is relevant to us as business owners and leaders today.

Remember the last time you bought a houseplant. Over time, you feed and water it, and even give it a bigger pot, so it will continue to grow and thrive. If you have seen me on-line recently you will know I have a Ficus tree that is rapidly taking over my offic

Now imagine you never water it - we all know what will happen - the plant will wither and die. This basic and universal principle is described in The Second Law of Thermodynamics.

THE SCIENCE BIT

I will summarise, if you want to go 'full science' check out Wikipedia.

The Second Law of Thermodynamics states that "in any closed system, without any external input, entropy will increase". For entropy, read decay.

Basically, this means everything decays over time unless there is some sort of external action. This is why food decays, cars rust, buildings crumble, humans age, the waste in our landfill sites will decay (even though it will take thousands of years), our Sun will eventually go out, etc. I think you get the picture...

One of the most fascinating facts about this Law is that there are no exceptions - there are no examples of decay in reverse - I bet you can't think of any!

WHY IS THIS RELEVANT?

Imagine you have now, or you take on a role as a leader or manager, or you buy or start a business, and you spend all your time just being in your role, job or business. This is exactly like bringing a houseplant home and never watering it - but wait I hear you say - We have team reviews and team meetings, we plan, we set goals, we market our business, we attract customers etc, etc. But - you are not watering or feeding your role or business, you **are just letting it get on with the day-to-day activities and operations** of your job or business.

The Second Law states that, without external intervention, entropy (decay) will increase.

Here are some examples of what you already know happens in businesses and organisations without external input:

1. Job dissatisfaction increases, people resign, people feel undervalued and are de-motivated.

2. Processes which once were fit for purpose become less and less effective because demands, particularly in technology, increase.

3. Profitability decreases as costs increase because we try to do more and more with what we have.
4. Products and services which were once cutting edge and relevant to your market become second best in your market because your competitors are innovating and investing.

WHAT'S THE SOLUTION?

As a responsible business owner, I know that if I am to stay ahead of natural decay, I must implement a strategy that supports a level of innovation and investment that is higher than the natural rate of decay.

Without a level of investment which out-performs natural decay, your role, your team, your business or organisation, will inevitably decay. We all know the only constant in life is change. Unless you are investing in positive change, negative change is inevitable.

*I use the term geek in a light-hearted way and as "a knowledgeable enthusiast or intellectual".

See also
Possibilities and Probabilities? (p133)
The Perpetual Motion Business (p215)
What Does Packard's Law Teach Us About Business Growth? (p223)

Mark's Three Principles For Success

Invest your time into these three principles and your success will be easier.

1. Invest time in your people
2. Invest quality in your quantity
3. Invest money in your future

Investing time in your people will build strong relationships and bring you what you want, not more of what you already get.

Investing quality in your quantity will ensure your business is growing with an infinite mindset, always working towards better, and keeping you at the top of your game.

Investing money in your future will keep you focussed on what you do best, bring your vision into focus, and create the future you always wanted.

These principles apply to any business, of any size or any age.

Get The Jarvis Principles free from my website:

www.mark-jarvis.co.uk

What Are Big Goals And What Are Ordinary Goals?

Firstly, I will say any goal is good because it provides focus and helps us work towards a future we have crafted.

Is it not also true, though, that we are, if we are serious about growth, whether personal or professional, always setting ourselves goals in some shape or other?

We may set ourselves goals which look like:

- I want to grow my business.
- I want to run a marathon.
- I want to be the best at…
- I want to spend more time with the family.
- I want to eat more healthily.
- I want to be happier.
- I want to make more money.
- I want to grow my team.

All good goals, but are they big goals? I would suggest not. These are ordinary goals, not because they are any less valuable, but because **once achieved, we have to go on and set another goal, and another, and another**.

When I'm working with clients, we work on a 5-year vision, 3-year goals and a 1-year plan.

This brings real focus and builds traction and momentum, they and it are ever evolving and growing towards their big goals.

A big goal, or BHAG (Big Hairy Audacious Goal) as is often quoted, is a goal that changes our lives, something that, once achieved, will mean we can and will move on to the next chapter in our lives.

For many, we say that achieving our goals is down to willpower, however… Big goals negate the need for willpower because **the excitement of the dream goal drives us into action.**

When we live every single day with a vision in our minds of the actuality of that dream, we are so busy moving towards our big goal and chasing what we believe is possible we just don't have time for fear, blame and thoughts that hold us back.

Do you have a big goal or BHAG?

What's your 5 year vision?

See also
Possibilities and Probabilities? (p133)
What Does Making Changes In Business Really Mean? (p163)
Why Are My Clients Not Held Accountable? (p153)

What Trust Should Be

Charles Blondin, the French tightrope walker is famous for many acrobatic acts of daring do. He is perhaps most famous for crossing the Niagara gorge over 300 times. And, on occasion, doing so with some amazing props, including crossing with a wheelbarrow, and making an omelette halfway across. Probably most famous, though, is his act of carrying a man across the gorge.

This is a quite incredible act of daring and risk taking, but also shows an incredible amount of faith and belief in himself and his ability to complete the task. Whilst we may think that one of his acts of daring may have been his downfall, actually he survived well into his 60's and was still wowing the crowds until complications following diabetes took him.

What interests me most is not his complete faith and belief in himself, but how he was able to convince somebody to jump on his back and be carried across a gorge of over 1100 ft with a raging torrent below.

I wonder how much belief, faith and trust I would need to have in somebody for me to jump on their back and be carried across a gorge on a tightrope!!

Of course, there has to be a message in there for us today…

What is it that makes us believe and trust in ourselves to do what we need to do to fulfil our vision. At what point do we choose to seek the support of another, and **at what** point do we have an unwavering faith in that person to be able to help and support us to get to where we want to be in life and business in the same way that the man who was carried across Niagara Falls had faith in Charles Blondin.

TRUST IS HAVING FAITH IN THE INTEGRITY OF OTHERS

We are all aware of the concept of Know, Like and Trust. I believe trust comes not just from us consistently demonstrating our trustworthiness, but at a higher and even more profound level, it comes from integrity.

We build trust by interacting with others, and our trustworthiness relies on how others see us, so **trust is based on the perspective of others**. I wonder why we are so fixated on building trust with others when what we should be focussed on is integrity (faith in trusting ourselves).

Integrity is different because it does not rely on others, it is fundamental to our very being and is about what we are. **Trust can be built; integrity is something we have** (or don't have).

Does your desire to grow your business come from a commercially driven series of activities designed to build trust and convert prospects into clients, or does your desire to grow yourself and your business come from your profound faith and belief in your integrity.

For me, **integrity is not about who we are, what we've done, our achievements or accolades, but what we are when no-one is looking**.

See also
How To Unlock The Power Of Focus (p85)
Be, Do, Have - What Does It Mean? (p107)
Know, Like, Trust - What Does It Really Mean? (p193)

Possibilities And Probabilities

It's true that our waking day is spent thinking about possibilities and 'what if's'.

Most of our wishes, hopes and aspirational thoughts are around positive possibilities and most of our worries and stressful thoughts are around negative possibilities.

It's also true that we are hard-wired for survival so negative possibilities almost always win out - it is part of the basic fight or flight reactio

Here's where probability kicks in; the more we think about and focus on what's possible, positive or negative, the more we believe it's probable. The more probable we believe a possibility will be, the more likely that will become our reality - think about this for a moment… (I hope your brain hasn't exploded!)

Just thinking about your business, your aims and goals, and by focussing on what's possible makes those goals and aims become more probable and therefore a reality.

LET'S THINK ABOUT DECISION MAKING

The most difficul action to take is deciding to take action, not what action to take.

WHAT DOES THAT MEAN IN REALITY?

I've found the more you focus on what might go wrong, what might not work, what your naysayers tell you, and what your competitors might do first, the more likely those possibilities are to become your reality, just because you are thinking it's more probable.

HOW TO TURN IT AROUND

I know it's easy to say, but focus on positive possibilities. Believe in your goals, stay true to your aims, your vision, your values and purpose.

Once upon a time you thought you couldn't run a business, now look where you are!

Focus on what your life and business could look like when all your positive possibility becomes probable, and it will become real.

The challenge is in making the decision. Don't let negative possibilities hold you back, decide to change by focussing on one positive possibility today and seek support and help to make that possibility a reality.

"If you think you can or if you think you can't, either way you're right" - Henry Ford.

See also*:*
How To Avoid The Catch When Finding Your Purpose (p11)
Getting The Business Basics Right - 8 Tips For Success (p61)
How To Unlock The Power Of Focus (p85)
Be, Do, Have - What Does It Mean? (p107)
What Are Big Goals And What Are Ordinary Goals? (p129)

The Reality Of Referrals In Business

I've been sharing my insights into the concept of 'referrals for better business' for several years now and I thought it was about time I shared them with you too.

I thought I would do this by way of relaying a conversation I have regularly when discussing marketing and sales strategies.

I've taken the fluff out and just given you the juicy bits, and I would like you to think, 'If this were me, where would I sit in this conversation (what level would I be)?'

I'll give you a bit of context first; John owns and runs a serviced based business, with a team of 7 (at the time of writing, it's grown since then), serving the B2B market in the UK.

The conversation begins like this:

Me - How do you feel about referrals in business?

John - Yes, well, obviously they're good, I actually get quite a lot of referrals.

Me - That's great, may I ask who refers you?

John - Mostly my customers and sometimes a few from networking events I attend.

I call this LEVEL 1 simply because its where most people are if they've been in business at least a couple of years. They are building a network, they have some customers, and they are becoming known for what they do. Let's continue the conversation....

Me - How often do people refer you?

John - Not sure really, they just refer when they can I suppose.

Me - How does that make you feel?

John - Great, obviously. It feels really good when someone refers me out of the blue.

Me - Would you agree then that for the majority of the time, some of your customers refer you sometimes?

John - Yes, I would agree with that.

Me - How would you feel if your customers referred you more of the time?

John - Yes, obviously it would be better but it's not going to happen in reality, is it?

Me - May I ask, how much time and money are you currently spending looking for and getting new business?

John - Quite a lot probably, I don't really know to be honest.

Me - What if you include the time you spend networking and on social media, would that be even more time?

John - Yes it would.

Me - What if I showed you how you could have a strategy and plan in place so more of your customers are referring you more of the time, how important would it be for you to know how to do that?

John - Sounds good in principle, I'm interested to know, not sure if I've got the time or money to do that though.

Me - You've already said that what you're currently doing to gain new business costs you a lot, my question would be, what's it costing you not to have a plan to get more of your customers referring you more of the time? What are you giving up at the expense of being busy?

John - A fair point I suppose......

NOTE, at this point the conversation goes into what better engagement with customers might look like, including follow up conversations and even just asking for recommendations and referrals. I'm sure you can see it's a very bespoke and personal approach so I'm just giving you the highlights so you can see what the reality is for referrals in business today.

Now, with a plan and strategy in place for communication, networking and conversation we are **at LEVEL 2 and more of our customers are referring us more of the time.**

LET'S CONTINUE THE CONVERSATION...

Me - Earlier you mentioned that you also get some referrals from your network. When did that last happen?

John - Actually it was just last week, someone from my networking group called me and introduced me to someone who needed their xxx reviewing.

Me - Has that turned into business yet?

John - not yet, sometimes it takes a while because of (what I do).

Me - Of course, I appreciate that. When was the last time you remember a referral from your network turning into business?

John - Probably a few weeks ago, not sure really, just thinking, why do you ask?

Me - I'm interested to know a couple of things really, first, how often these referrals turn into business for you, and second, how much less time you invest in converting that referral.

John - Well, mostly they turn into business….

Me - Just to be clear, do you mean most of the time or some of the time?

John - I would say some of the time.

Me - Ok, so how much less time does it take you to convert those referrals?

John - Obviously it takes less time, usually there's still some work to do but on the whole, I think it's working well.

LEVEL 3 is where most people are when they are part of a network, where some people bring referrals and introductions some of the time, but it's still not consistent or predictable.

Me - What if I showed you not only how to get **more of your customers referring you more of the time but also get your network referring you more of the time?** Do you think you could cope with that increase in business?

John - Good question, if I'm honest, you make a good point and if I was getting more referrals from customers and my network, plus the usual enquiries… mmm, good question.

Now, with a strategy and plan which also includes **more referrals from more of our network, we are at LEVEL 4.** Again, at this point the conversation goes into what that plan might look like. To give you an idea, we talked about improving John's presentations which made it easier for his colleagues to create introductions, and we talked about making more of his story which in turn made it more straightforward for his colleagues to recommend him.

FOR NOW, LET'S CONTINUE THE CONVERSATION...

Me - We've already talked about how much time and money you spend gaining new customers and how you could change that, may I ask what your thoughts are regarding growing your business? Are you busy at the moment?

John - Yes, pretty busy, could always do with more though right (laughs).

Me - Of course, that's why we're all here. So, would a few more customers mean that you're diary remains full?

John - Yes, I suppose so.

Me - If your diary is mostly full all of the time, how will you grow your business if you can't be busier?

John - (smiles) You've got some good questions haven't you! Ok, honestly? I don't know. I suppose I would have to start thinking about employing another team member.

Me - So you're going to employ another person just to make them as busy as you and the rest of the team are?

John - Yes, I suppose so, what else is there, that's it isn't it?

Me - I don't think it is and here's why; most businesses grow by expansion as described - get busy, expand, get busy, expand etc. The problem with that is whilst it's a perfectly viable way to grow a business and you will increase your turnover, you are also typically increasing your costs. I believe this is a finite business growth strategy because time is finite

What we are not addressing is profits. By focussing on profits, we have a way to grow infinitely because the potential for profit is infinite. **What would it mean to you if you were focussing on profit in your business not just gaining clients and being busy?**

John - I hadn't really thought of it that way, I guess I really am focussing on more business.

Me - We've already talked about a plan for more referrals, both from your customers and your network. How about we now think about better referrals. Would you agree that, if you were to get better quality referrals, referrals for higher revenue business and more enjoyable business, you could be in a position to make more money in less time?

John - When you put it like that, yes, it makes an awful lot of sense, really helpful....

Now, with a strategy and plan in place which also includes referrals for better, not just more business, we're focussing on **building a more profitable business and we are at LEVEL 5**. This final level is about where you are taking your business next. Not just focussing on more of the same business you are already getting, but identifying and moving into new markets, perhaps with new products and services, and to do this John needed to re-educate his network on what he wanted next.

As mentioned, I'd really like to know which level you think you're at, here's the levels again.

Once you've decided you want to move up, give me a call and I will show you how.

Level 1 - Most people are in this position because referrals happen by accident, some of their customers refer them some of the time, they think it's going well but they are unaware of what they are leaving on the table.

Level 2 - They have a strategy and plan in place so that more of their customers are referring them more of the time.

Level 3 - Most people who have begun to build a network are in this position. Some of their network refer them some of the time, but it's still not consistent or predictable.

Level 4 - The strategy and plan now also includes more referrals from more of their network.

Level 5 - Better not just more. Your network is referring you regularly for what you want not what you are already getting, ie the business you want next which supports the potential for infinite growth in profit

Which level are you, and where would you like to be?

See also
How To Avoid The Catch When Finding Your Purpose (p11)
What Trust Should Be (p131)
Why Aren't You More Profitable In Your Network? (p149)
How Do You Know If Those In Your Network Are The Right People? (p159)
Which Came First, The Sales Pipeline Or The Relationship Pipeline? (p167)
Know, Like, Trust - What Does It Really Mean? (p193)
The Top Seven Barriers To Consistent Quality Referrals (p203)

The Two Most Powerful Questions In Business

Ask yourself these two incredibly powerful questions to get to the crux of your business needs

1. **What do you want to be known for?**

As the leader, owner or founder of a business, working out what you want to be known for is a pretty straight forward task, simply brainstorm your why, your vision and your mission. Get these statements written up and they will form the core of your marketing messages.

Please don't underestimate the importance of these messages for your business, I've worked with so many who were just working on what they do rather than why they do it.

Once you've worked out what you want to be known for and this message is going out in everything you do, say and be, you can ask the next question...

2. **What are you actually known for?**

I have found the gap between what you want to be known for and what you are actually known for is one of the biggest barriers to growth for businesses now and in the future. It hasn't always been that way, but I firmly believe it is now and will be.

When the answer to those two questions match, you're on the right track. Remember - people don't buy what you do, they buy why you do it.

What do you think you are known for?

Dunbar's Number And Why You Should Care

In the 1990s anthropologist and evolutionary psychologist Robin Dunbar postulated that the number of relationships that any one person can maintain is based on the size of their brain, in this case the neocortex. Since humans have the largest brain of any mammal it makes sense then that they are best equipped to manage the most number of relationships.

WHY YOU SHOULD CARE ABOUT THE NUMBER 150

Dunbar further says in his research that the maximum number of stable relationships any one person can maintain is 150, beyond this, factions appear.

Let's take a moment to think about how this number has impacted our world and driven our evolution, here's a quick example.

From our earliest days, humans have built communities based on 150, from stone age villages, through mediaeval times, villages have, on average, topped out at around 150.

When that number is exceeded, a new community is formed. That's why, from our earliest days, the human population has been brought together in many thousands of small communities. When villages become towns, you will find sub-communities within those towns, in larger cities you will find townships or suburbs. You are probably living in one of these right now. Even our postal system is based on street name, community name, town or city name.

RELATIONSHIPS NOT CONNECTIONS

In our modern world it would be very easy to dismiss the number 150 as something which is no longer relevant. **Our digital world now allows us to connect globally to tens of thousands, even millions of people without ever leaving our home.** This is a great opportunity for us to expand our connections, but please remember, **these are not relationships they are just connections.**

Our social media world encourages us to make more and more connections, these are not relationships. It will take another evolutionary leap forward in the size of our brain for us to maintain more than 150 relationships, I have commented in previous articles that we have only had access to computers, the internet and even the telephone for **less than one thousandth of our evolutionary journey** in time.

IT'S SCIENCE, EMBRACE IT, DON'T FIGHT IT

Let me show you some maths, don't worry it's easy!

There is a very simple formula which shows how many relationships exist in a group of any given number, here's the formula:

(N x N-1) / 2 = R

Where R is relationships and N is the number of people in the group.

LET'S PUT SOME NUMBERS ON THAT

Imagine a group of 6 people - (6 x 5) / 2 = 15 Relationships.

How about a group of 10 - (10 x 9) / 2 = 45 Relationships.

How about an average family size of 14 - (14 x 13) / 2 = 91 Relationships.

I know what you're thinking…

15 - that's easy.

45 - ok, so I think I'm happy managing 45 relationships.

91 - so now I'm feeling a little under pressure thinking about how I can cope with 91 different levels of conversation, communication and relationship. **You are feeling that because it's a biological reaction.**

I'm sure you can see where this is going.

Just to be clear, the number of relationships to be maintained is not only the number of relationships that you have directly within other individuals, but you also need to maintain an understanding of the relationships between the other people in the group, and you.

In business terms, I have found that our natural number is 12. 12 people with whom we have 66 strong business relationships.

YOU SHOULD CARE BECAUSE…

As I've been saying for a long time, **relationships not connections drive our world**, whether in business or personally. If you want to build a strong sustainable business, you need to build your relationships. You need to grow your network, up to a certain point (the Dunbar number), and you need to **cultivate those relationships, so they become strong and deep relationships not superficial connections**.

To leverage the power of your network you need to tap into the relationships you have and develop them into business generating opportunities. You need to know that more is not better, more it's just faster and more diluted.

Strength and depth have and will always work more effectively in the long run. Put simply, it's evolutionary silence, don't fight it

See also
Why Aren't You More Profitable In Your Network? (p149)
How Do You Know If Those In Your Network Are The Right People? (p159)
Are You Working In Transaction World Or Relationship World? (p235)

Why Defining Your Target Market Shouldn't Be So Hard

I've spent many years helping businesses identify their Target Market and when asking, I've found that most answer by saying, "Well, I can do business with anyone…" and whilst it may be true that we can do business in any industry, particularly if we have a service-based business, I believe it's not true that we want and should do business with anyone.

After all, I'm sure we've all spent time with clients who we subsequently wish we had not engaged.

After spending many years myself in that exact position, i.e. thinking about which industries I want to work with, I had a revelation!

What if we did business with the right people first and think about industries afterwards? With this approach we immediately remove drama, reduce time and money objections and have the best clients.

Would you rather work with nice clients or every client?

I decided to work with nice clients and I'm sure you would, too, if you're not already.

When doing business by relationship and with the right people, you CAN still do business in any industry, you will just be doing business with the right people, those who share your values and beliefs.

I believe the most successful businesses recognise that **better business makes more profit than just more business.**

WHAT SHOULD YOU DO FIRST?

For you to attract nice clients, you need to know what nice looks like for you.

Here's three things you should have in place in your business:

1. Know and understand why you do what you do.
2. Define and share your values
3. A credible Vision and Mission.

See also
How To Avoid The Catch When Finding Your Purpose (p11)
Why Start-Ups Sometimes Fail (p57)
Make It Better Before Trying To Make It Bigger (p103)

Why Aren't You More Profitable In Your Network?

One of the most frequent questions I get is "How can I get more business from my network?" So, I thought I would share with you some insights into Visibility, Credibility and Profitabilit .

This is a process we all go through as we build relationships and is fundamental to creating a flow of regular referrals in our business.

FIRSTLY, LETS DEFINE THE THREE ELEMENTS:
1. **Visibility**: This is when people know you and they know what you do, for example, when you attend a networking event and there are several people in the room who know you by name. A good measure of this is when you don't need to pass business cards to those people as they already know what you do.
2. **Credibility:** This is when people know you and they know what you do, and they know you are good at what you do. Typically, your current customer base should fit into this bracket. However, you can be credible with people without doing business with them. To be credible with people you haven't done business with you will need to have a strong relationship with them and, more often than not, have helped them either personally or in their business, perhaps in a non-transactional way. Building credibility with people often means sharing

personal information with them, perhaps family, favourite places to go on holiday, hobbies etc.

3. **Profitability**: This is when people know who you are, know what you do, they know you're good at what you do, and they're willing to recommend you to other people. This final stage can be the foundation for a truly profitable referral-based business. Being recommended to a new customer by an existing customer can be a very powerful introduction and we all know how great it feels to receive this level of introduction.

Success in your network is not just about being visible with the people you meet. To truly build a profitable network you need to go through all three stages and build strong relationships with your referral partners.

HERE'S SOME ADDITIONAL POINTS TO NOTE:

You can be at different levels with different people and a good exercise to go through with your current network is to categorise each of your network connections in terms of Visibility, Credibility and Profitabilit . Once you know what level you're at with each of your connections, you can begin to work on those relationships to move them towards Profitabilit .

For those of you who are members of networking groups or clubs, please note that simply asking for introductions to people is unlikely to work until you're credible with the people you're asking, so building credibility is a vital step which must not be overlooked.

There is one final point which I'd like to make: to add in another word within Visibility, Credibility and Profitabilit . This word is **Regularity**. I believe to be credible with someone you need to be regularly visib**le with them, and to be profitable with someone you need to be regularly credible with them.**

As you can see, profitability is not a short-term process it is a long-term referral marketing strategy which can win your company massive amounts of business by building strong relationships and credibility with the people in your network.

See also
What trust should be (p131)
The reality of referrals in business today (p135)
Dunbar's number and why you should care (p143)
How do you know if those in your network are the right people? (p159)
Which came first, the sales pipeline or the relationship pipeline? (p167)

Mark Jarvis

Why Are My Clients Not Held Accountable?

Accountability without desire fuels failure. 'What?' I hear you ask, I thought that was what business mentors and coaches do. Actually, it's not, but that's for another day.

Very rarely will you hear me talk about accountability as a feature or benefit - I know many do, but not me. You won't find mention of accountability anywhere on my website and in the programmes, training and courses I run through the Academy for Scaling Businesses, and here's why.

When was the last time you had to be held accountable for booking your next holiday or buying your partner a birthday or anniversary gift? How about watching your favourite TV program or taking a day to pursue your favourite hobby?

Why don't you need to be held accountable for these and other things? Simply because the desire or willingness to act is so strong, there is no need for any conscious focus.

Why then is taking decisive action in business so difficul that so many people keep talking about accountability? For me, the answer is simple. Unless you have the desire to act, no amount of accountability is ever going to make a lasting and significant difference and create chang

Whatever your role, position, age or size of business, you will at some point reach your limits. To solve this, some seek more information, some undertake endless training and courses, and some put in place peer to peer or individual accountability steps in the vague hope it will create desire - it won't.

Do you lead or manage a team where you are trying to focus your team to act and are putting feedback and accountability steps in place in order to get the work done?

Instead, inspire your team to desire change - how to inspire change is beyond the scope of these notes (it's what the Academy for Scaling Businesses is all about).

HUMANS ARE HARD-WIRED TO RESIST CHANGE

Yet change is very often the one thing we seek when thinking about growth.

You want to grow yourself and scale your business, but you are not willing enough to change such that accountability becomes irrelevant.

Some people believe the grass is greener on the other side of the fence if only they could get over there and enjoy it. It's not enough to find a ladder, or even put the ladder next to the fence - YOU have to climb it!

See also
Why Creative Distraction Is Holding You Back (p65)
Make It Better Before Trying To Make It Bigger (p103)
Is Today Your Last Groundhog Day? (p117)
What Are Big Goals And What Are Ordinary Goals? (p129)
Possibilities and Probabilities (p133)

Plan For Increased Productivity Through Professional Networking

This article is about the process of assessing and developing your professional network so you are able to effectivel develop yourself and your business. It is a methodology that will create for you infinite developing opportunities.

This article is not in any way a measure of what makes a good or poor professional network or networking group. Every networking group, without exception, provides value and opportunity and it is up to us as individuals and businesses to make sure we are working the formula to its best effect

Here I will share with you the **Five Steps of Assessment** you can use in your professional networking activities so you can access the networks of others to reach your target market, whatever that may be now, and whatever you may want it to be in the future.

This methodology applies each time you want to take a growth step in your business. Before we begin, there are two points to note:

1. Most professional networks contain people with 'random access to your target market'. By this I mean they do business and refer business when the need or opportunity arises. A group of people with 'regular access to your target market' is the beginning of an effective Referral Marketing Strategy and is beyond

the scope of this chapter. When you are ready for this pinnacle level, please contact me.

2. Social networking. Again, the scope of this article excludes us from exploring the value social networking brings. This style of network, whilst still professional, is most often characterised as having a strong community or social service element.

THE FIVE STEPS OF ASSESSMENT

When participating in a professional network, ask yourself these questions;

1. Can I do business directly with the people here?
2. Can these people introduce or refer me to others?
3. Will these people take action, either directly with me, or indirectly on my behalf?
4. Do these people have reach into my target market?
5. Are these people credible in their own target market?

Let's explore the implications of each of these steps, and how you can plan to increase your productivity through professional networking.

If you are currently answering 'yes' at least to the first two or three, you are probably in the right place for what you want now.

Step 1 - Needs little explanation I feel and is where most people begin. Simply put, do these people have a product or service I need now or in the future, and do I have a product or service they need or want. You may notice this style of network has a high turnover, is low impact, and is primarily transactional.

Step 2 - Most people have a desire to help each other. My advice is to make sure you are investing enough time with your colleagues so they have a full understanding of who you are, what you stand for and what you do. Only when others understand you, will they be able to introduce you.

You may notice this style of network often has a formula which encourages one to one time with fellow members.

Step 3 - Being completely honest, neither Step 1 or Step 2 matter if we cannot answer 'yes' with conviction, to Step 3. I have found the biggest barrier to Step 3 is trust. We may have a full understanding of what each other does, but if trust does not exist, no amount of knowledge is going to motivate you to act on someone's behalf. The answer? Constantly and consistently deliver on your promises both explicit and implied.

Step 4 - This level unlocks infinite growth. Each step in the evolution of your business, each time you want to open new markets, have a new product or service to offe , you should ask the Step 4 question. It may be the networks in which you participate do have reach into your new target market, but it may not always be the case.

One of the most obvious 'red flags' for me is when we begin to find it a challenge to sell our new product into our current market, we often end up reducing our prices to match our network when in fact **we should be finding a new network to match our prices**. This is one of several key mindset changes needed to unlock infinite growth

Step 5 - Credibility, ours and that of others, has to be one of our top priorities. I have briefly explored trustworthiness in Step 3 and in all our professional networks we must have a level of credibility our prospects cannot question. If those we are asking to introduce and refer us are not credible themselves, the opportunities for business we are asking for will never materialise, or at the very least, be equally time and resource hungry as any usual transaction in our business.

I hope by sharing these insights, I have shown you a way for you to use professional networking as a way to support the growth, expansion and evolution of your business.

Remember, it may not be just your target market which is evolving, it can just as easily be your own personal development. Either way, I have found these five steps to always provide a sound basis for the continuing assessment of our professional networking activities.

See also
What Trust Should Be (p131)
The Reality Of Referrals In Business (p135)
Why Aren't You More Profitable In Your Network? (p149)
How Do You Know If Those In Your Network Are The Right People? (p159)
Know, Like, Trust - What Does It Really Mean? (p193)

How Do You Know If Those In Your Network Are The Right People?

I am often asked about how to build the right network. The question often starts with "How do I network?' or "Where should I network?" and if you haven't already, please read *How To Plan For Increased Productivity Through Networking (page 155)*, essentially Part 1 to this Part 2.

Professional networking is so much more than simply finding and participating in the right networking groups - it's a good place to start, but it's not the final solution.

Much like the famous quote by Jim Rohn, *"You are the average of the five people you spend the most time with"*, the key to building a successful business lies in the people you have around you both in your team and in your network. Building a productive network starts with having the right people around you.

Here are my two golden rules to discover who are the right people to have in your network.

1. **You can tell them bad news and they will just listen**. They won't judge you or try to fix you or tell you why they had the same experience, and it was worse. Most importantly, you won't feel shame or guilt for sharing a failure.

2. **You can tell them good news and they will help you celebrate**. They won't make you feel guilty for your success, they won't congratulate you publicly on social media whilst secretly wishing it was them.

They won't immediately tell you about their success or the success of someone else they know.

You want to be around people who want the best for you. Those who encourage success in others, not those who want to piggy-back your success to be successful themselves.

It's acceptable and desirable to surround yourself with people who are facilitating your development. They listen and cooperate with you and help you move towards a better future.

If they don't pay any attention and they keep doing the same things over and over again, they are not going anywhere. If it's beginning to get painful, then it's time for you to move on. **They may be lovely people, but they are limiting your success with their own apathy**.

You have the right and responsibility to surround yourself with people who are good for the best part of you. Remember this when aligning yourself with those who are invested in your future.

See also
What Trust Should Be (p131)
How To Plan For Increased Productivity Through Professional Networking (p155)

Igniting Conversations

I've been thinking about how we have conversations, particularly in business meetings. This was prompted by a conversation I overheard whilst waiting for a meeting of my own. The conversation started in the normal way, with general greetings and chitchat, I won't go into the details of what was talked about for obvious reasons, but one of the things I noticed was the structure of the conversation and the way that we reply to questions and points raised by the other person.

Like me, I'm sure you have often found yourself listening intently to the other person whilst at the same time thinking about how you can offer a smart reply or a clever question. This, in fact, is the way that most of our conversations are held and is a learned technique.

What if there were a better way? A way to ignite conversations?

Sometimes I think it's very easy for our passion to take over in our business conversations. We all know the power of listening most and speaking least, but sometimes it's not always easy to do. Yesterday I had four meetings with four very different people, some mostly listening, some were mostly talking and some where a balance of both.

Which one do you think I enjoyed the most? Of course, it will be the conversations focussed more on listening.

Next time you find yourself in conversation, rather than focusing on your smart reply, clever question or your own perspective on their point, think about how you can respond in a way which reinforces their point, allows them to elaborate, gives you more information and helps them to increase their enthusiasm and passion for who they are.

Have conversations which ignite the passion held within all of us for who we are and why we do what we do. After all, I care less about what you do and what you've done, and much much more about how you make me feel.

See also
How Do You Know If Those In Your Network Are The Right People? (p159)
How To Keep Your Battery Charged (p187)
Which Question I Am Asked Most Often (p209)

What Does Making Changes In Business Really Mean?

First, I need to ask a question to help you understand the differen e between change which creates a solution and change which makes you busy.

Is your goal to get a solution which fixes your challenges forever, or do you want something which makes you feel better about yourself because you are busy doing something differently?

I started my career journey in the hotel and hospitality industry, and in the late 1980s I was organising and managing all sorts of different events from weddings and shows to corporate conferences. One common factor that exists in pretty much any event is the lunchtime queue. I'm sure you've done it yourself the last time you attended an event, the speeches are over, the presentations are finished and the host says, 'OK, now ladies and gentlemen we're going to break for lunch', and everybody piles over to the buffet where we form an orderly queue and wait our turn, ready to fill our plate with all that's on off .

I'm sure you remember that lunch and the queue you joined, and whilst it's nice to chat with others, we all wish we could get to the front as quickly as possible.

Why was there a queue? Typically because the catering arrangements were laid out in such a way that people queued from one end and filled their plate as they move along the buffet to finally collect their beautifully wrapped knives and forks and return to their table to eat.

In so many cases, the catering facilities have always traditionally been arranged at the side of the room with one side of the tables against the wall, and people queuing along the buffet to collect their food

I remember starting a particular contract in the late 1980s where I had to ask the question. Why are people queuing at the buffet in only one direction? Why can't we move the buffet to the middle of the room, and have people use the buffet on both sides. In fact, why can't we have multiple food stations where there is no need to queue at all.

The changes we made to the way we ran our events and provided the catering gave our clients a better experience.

Change is about creating a different result, not about creating a list of things to change.

What we created was a solution that changed the outcome for the people we served. This brings us back to the original question. What does it mean to make a change in business. For me, change is about creating something that changes the results. It's not about creating a change in activity just for the sake of doing or trying something differentl .

Next time you are thinking about making changes in your business, think about what I did when I was in the hotel industry in the 1980s and move your buffet to the middle of the room. **Take action that results in change and creates a better outcome for those you serve.**

The results you create for your business, customers and clients should not just be different, they should be better.

Sometimes you don't need to change the world. Perhaps making just one or two small changes which fix your challenges forever might be the very thing you are looking for.

Think about what will make a difference to the output of your business, whether its customer service, a new product, or a product used in a different wa .

If it makes your output better, then this is the change to make.

See also
Make It Better Before Trying To Make It Bigger (p103)
What Are Big Goals And What Are Ordinary Goals? (p129)
Possibilities and Probabilities (p133)

Invest Time In Your People

Investing time in your people will build strong relationships and bring you what you want... not more of what you already have.

No matter what technological trends distract us, people and how we work with them will always matter most.

Whether you are inspiring your team, delegating responsibility, investing in training or simply being the leader you should be... People matter first

Whether you are engaging with customers, suppliers, building your team or your network, demonstrating authenticity builds trust. Investing time in your people to help them, support them or simply guide them will ensure you are all working consistently to be better.

Which Came First, Sales Pipeline Or The Relationship Pipeline?

Common knowledge suggests the Sales Pipeline came first, after all, how can you build a relationship with a client unless they've been in your Sales Pipeline, right? Common knowledge also suggests that to create a sale we spend time, energy and money building a relationship with the prospect to then convert them into a client.

It is true that the traditional sales pipeline consists of:

1. Some sort of acquisition activity (marketing, social media, networking etc).
2. A number of steps designed to build confidence in you, your product or service.
3. Some sort of objection handling process.
4. Some sort of closing or converting process.

The fundamental truth is that all of those things cost time, energy and money, and each time you go through the process, it costs you more.

WHAT IS A RELATIONSHIP PIPELINE?

The most important thing to know is a Relationship Pipeline creates referrals not sales. Sales is what your Sales Pipeline does (or doesn't depending on how much it costs you).

In a Sales Pipeline, it takes approximately **20 connections/ leads to create 1 client.**

In a Relationship Pipeline, it takes just **one person to refer you forever.**

Put the right people in your Relationship Pipeline and you will have more referrals than you can handle. I know which one I prefer, and I know which one is my top priority.

84 IS A SCARY NUMBER!

Did you know, on average, it takes 8 hours of work to gain a client?

Did you know it takes almost the same amount of time to not get a client?

Let's say in the traditional Sales Pipeline, your one client has cost you 8 hours of work.

Let's say the other 19 leads you had which didn't turn into business still cost you 4 hours each.

The total cost in time, energy and money for one client is now 1x8hrs plus 19x4hrs.

Total time cost = **84hrs - Did you know this about your business?**

WHY YOUR RELATIONSHIP PIPELINE SHOULD COME FIRST

Put simply, I invest in one relationship to generate referrals forever, for every person I have in my Relationship Pipeline, I have the opportunity to attract my ideal client at the right time and with the right budget.

For every 8hrs I invest in my Relationship Pipeline, I have the opportunity for infinite referrals. For every 8hrs I invest in my Sales Pipeline, I have the opportunity for one sale.

Having an active and effective Relationship Pipeline is a perfect example of an 'infinite game". Do please read Simon Sinek's book, *The Infinite Game* for'an in-depth study of the finite and infinite mindse

THE PUNCH LINE

What if I told you the referrals you are currently getting are not really referrals at all, they are just leads with a different name. Why? Because you still have to go through 90% of your sales process to convert that referral. This costs you time, energy and money every time.

Real referrals go into your sales pipeline 95% closed, leaving you just 5% of the work to do.

I'll ask you this simple question, **do you want to do 95% of the work, or 5% of the work?**

Do you just want more business, or do you really want better business, and are you prepared to take action and do something about your life and business, forever.

Make your conversation about a 5% solution?

See also
The Reality Of Referrals In Business Today (p135)
Why Aren't You More Profitable In Your Network? (p149)
The Top Seven Barriers To Consistent Quality Referrals (p203)
Are You Working In Transaction World Or Relationship World? (p235)

Mark Jarvis

What Is Customer Service Really?

To begin answering the question of 'What is customer service?' I'm going to draw on my 17+ years of experience in the hotel and hospitality industry.

Why do we focus so much of our money, time and energy on customer service, the simple answer is because customer service is, in reality, reputation management. When someone comes to my hotel, I want customers to have an amazing experience, come back again and again, and tell all their friends.

It seems strange then that so many choose to invest so little in the very people who are responsible for the organisation's most precious asset - reputation.

Have you ever taken a moment to think about how you decide on where to celebrate a family birthday or other celebration. Perhaps it might be a local restaurant. Perhaps the decision-making process might go something like this:

You talk with your family discussing which restaurant to go to, and whilst the discussion may start with the quality of food, often the ultimate decision is based on the quality of service.

Obviously if the food is rubbish, you're not going to go, if the service was rubbish, you're definitely not going to go, even if the food was great.

For me service and reputation are about culture and values and no matter how great your product, it's about what other people say about you (not your product) when you are not there that truly creates the recipe for success. **If you nurture a culture of quality, then quality will be the one thing that finds you.**

Richard Branson said, "If you look after your staff (or team), they will look after your customers."

You could easily add to this, "…and your customers will look after your business."

Now let's swap out some of those nouns, let's change staff to network and let's change customers to referrals. Now we have a quote that reads, *"If you look after your network they will look after your referrals and your referrals will look after your business."*

It's very easy to see the link between reputation and customer service and the importance of investing in your staff and team, perhaps it's less easy to see why investing in your network is so important. If referrals are important to you, as is having a plan to generate more and better referrals, your only option is to invest in your network in the same way that you would invest in your staff to improve customer service.

See also
The Secret To Cultural Success In Business (p71)
Which Came First, The Sales Pipeline Or The Relationship Pipeline? (p167)
Know, Like, Trust - What Does It Really Mean? (p193)

What Makes A Great Footballer?

With each seasonal return of sport on TV, I happen upon a football game and whilst not an avid fan (I much prefer a big V8 and a racetrack), I often watch a game and am impressed by the skills of the players.

The one key skill that catches my eye is that during the game **players don't move to where the ball is, they move to where it's going to be**, and their skill is in arriving at the same place and time as the ball, part skill, part instinct, part training...

Of course, I can't resist using this analogy in business, so it got me thinking, particularly about the way we set goals (yes, another pun). We are always being told we should set goals and there are many books and workshops on how to set goals and plan for milestones along the way to achieve them.

WHAT IF SUCCESS COMES LESS FROM THE GOAL AND MORE FROM THE JOURNEY?

What if it's more about arriving at the same place and time as your goal?

This makes us less fixated on the goal and more focussed on the journey or the activities to get us there.

Creating the best journey for ourselves, developing our skills, learning new tactics, perhaps making mistakes, taking advice and being kind to ourselves, is all part of the journey.

Like the football player who kicks the ball high into the air in the general direction of their team-mate who then must use their experience, skill, instinct, training and coaching to maintain control of the ball and pass it on. Perhaps business is all about playing the game and making the best of our journey (and creating a succession plan to pay on the business).

This plays (yes, another one) a big part in what motivates me, yes I can support and coach people to achieve their goals, but I've found that the real value, the real success, comes when making the journey successful.

The game of football is often called, 'The Beautiful Game' and perhaps the beauty is in playing the game and not winning the game. Could business be the same?

See also
What Are Big Goals And What Are Ordinary Goals? (p129)
Possibilities and Probabilities (p133)
It's Not The Ingredients, It's What You Do With Them (p185)

What Will You Let Go Of First?

When the time comes to sell your business, what do you think will be the first thing you let go?

Sales and Marketing?

Not if you are selling as a going concern, same for admin and staff.

How about your customers - will you let them go first

If you are going to just walk away after all those years of hard work, then a steady reduction in customers could be the answer, together with stopping your sales and marketing channels.

Most people who want to sell their business have a figure in mind that they think it's worth, but many have no idea how to develop an exit strategy to bring all the necessary elements together so their business has a value and future someone wants to buy.

The irony is every successful business or organisation has a business mentor or coach, yet it is often these many think they will let go of first.

Why?

Because many think the best way to sell their business is to cut costs, so their bottom line looks good to a buyer.

WHAT DO YOU THINK THE BUYER WANTS?

As someone who buys and invests in businesses, I want to see certainty, continuity, increasing profitability and a plan for growth. This will not happen if you have cut to a minimum your investment in activities that make a difference

What do you think will happen if something goes wrong during the sale process and you have let go of your help? You are on your own, and because certainty has reduced, your buyer may get cold feet or force you into unfavourable terms.

Don't be fooled into thinking that selling a business is easy, it's not. It is, however, simple if you know what and how to do it.

If you don't have an exit strategy for your business, or its still on your to-do list, talk to me and I will help you see if it's attractive enough to potential buyers - you still have time to fix it - and if you think you are going to easily sell for six, seven or eight-plus figures, you REALLY need to talk to someone who has actually sold SME's.

See also
How To Achieve The Second Goal Of Every Business Owner (p1)
Getting The Business Basics Right - 8 Tips For Success (p61)
Make It Better Before Trying To Make It Bigger (p103)
The 60:20:20 Rule (From The Jarvis Principles) (p197)
What's The Difference Between A Teacher, A Mentor And A Coach (p219)

Ten Ways To Say Thank You

It's amazing how far a simple 'thank you' can go. Research shows that customers spend more, employees accomplish more, and suppliers are more likely to raise their game, if they're thanked regularly.

"We're living in what I like to call the 'Thank You Economy,' because only the companies that can figure out how to mind their manners in a very old-fashioned way - and do it authentically - are going to have a chance of competing," says Gary Vaynerchuk author of *The Thank You Economy*,.

How exactly can you harness the power of appreciation? Here are ten ways to thank your customers, employees and suppliers to get you ahead.

1. BE SPECIFIC

Focus your gratitude on what the employee or suppliers actually did. Rather than saying, "Thanks for your good work," it would be more effective to say "Thanks for staying late last night to complete our project, your commitment really makes a difference to our team." Use a similar strategy with suppliers, recognise them when they go above and beyond what's expected.

Why it's important: A focused 'thank you' will be more meaningful and thus increase employees' motivation and productivity. A recent poll found that more than 35% of respondents consider lack of recognition of their work the biggest hindrance to productivity.

2. MAKE IT PERSONAL

Connecting your appreciation with the recipient's personal life can make your message more impactful. If you show gratitude with a gift, relating it to life beyond the business, can add substance to your 'thank you'.

Why it's important: Showing intimacy breaks the ice in an emotional, not just a professional way, and is the game-changing way to greater profits

3. MAKE IT OLD SCHOOL

When was the last time you received a handwritten 'thank you' note? In the era of social media, email and text messaging, it's likely been quite some time. Don't underestimate the impact of sending a note through the postal system.

Why it's important: Taking the time to write a thoughtful note indicates a deeper level of appreciation than simply dashing off a short email or text. Because the hand-written letter is pretty much a lost art, the extra effort will not go unnoticed and may make customers more inclined to give you repeat business or suppliers give you a better deal.

5. ADD SOME REAL VALUE

Host a customer appreciation day with deep discounts and giveaways for your loyal fans. Offer free delivery on all online orders. Give your employees small incentives for going above and beyond, like a gift certificate for a night at the movies or a small monetary or time bonus.

Why it's important: Sometimes words aren't enough. It's gestures such as these that in the long run can help boost your bottom line. If your customers feel you go out of your way to reward them, they're more likely to choose you over your less-appreciative competition.

6. DON'T FORGET THE LITTLE GUY

It's easy to remember and recognise the people you work with directly everyday. It's also important to give thanks to the often-overlooked crew who help your business run smoothly. Leave a thank you note for the cleaning team, give the courier a gift certificate to a local restaurant, or get a dozen cupcakes for others who supply your business regularly.

Why it's important: Most people don't thank these hard-working people. So, a little effort will make you stand out and can go a long way toward getting great service from these people.

7. REFER BUSINESS TO YOUR VENDORS AND PARTNERS

There may be no better way to thank your suppliers than by sending more business their way. While such a direct referral is always appreciated, you also could go a step further and host a party for all your suppliers and partners. Invite your suppliers, accountant, lawyer, investors and anyone else you do business with.

Why it's important: If you throw a party, you will not only be thanking your suppliers with a great time, but you'll also be giving everyone a chance to network and connect with new clients.

8. THINK OUTSIDE THE BOX

If you want to get the attention of suppliers and clients, send a distinctive thank-you gift. Consider geographically specific gifts - find out where your people are based and send them something from a local supplier.

Why it's important: Because some people receive hundreds of gifts throughout the year, you need to send a thank-you gift people will remember when it's time to pull out their wallets.

9. THANK YOUR COMPLAINING CUSTOMERS

Complaining customers are going out of their way to tell you why they're dissatisfied. This generally means they still want to do business with you, assuming you're able to fix the problem. When a customer complains, first thank them for their business and their feedback, then explain how you will make things right.

Why it's important: Most unhappy customers don't bother to complain, but simply take their business elsewhere. So every complaint should be seen as an opportunity to improve relationships and win repeat business.

10. GIVE SOCIAL MEDIA SHOUT-OUTS

Thank customers by posting on your feed and genuinely comment on their posts, which means a comment that supports their position and raises them up. Offer recommendations and share stories, and a thoughtful mention for loyal customers on social media publicly shows your gratitude. Feature one of your best clients on your company page, explaining why you appreciate them so much.

Why it's important: Some of your most loyal customers and brand advocates are online, so you should show how much you value them in the social media sphere where they interact most with you and your business.

For more ideas on how you can thank your employees, customers, suppliers and your wider network and set up a rewards system in your organisation, contact me at mark@mark-jarvis.co.uk

See also
The Secret To Cultural Success In Business (p71)
The Key To Organisational Health (p93)
Make It Better Before Trying To Make It Bigger (p103)
What Is Customer Service Really? (p171)

Five Key Ways To Build Customer Relationships

Money can't buy one of the most important things you need to promote your business: relationships. **How do customer relationships drive your business?** It's all about finding people who believe in your products or services. When it comes to tracking these people down, you have two choices:

You can do all the legwork yourself and spend big on marketing, but that's like rolling a boulder up a hill. You want to drive your business into new territory, but every step is hard and expensive. There's another less painful, and potentially more profitable wa ...

You can create an army to help you push that boulder up the hill instead. How do you do that? You develop relationships with people who don't just understand your particular expertise, product or service, but who are excited and buzzing about what you do. You stay connected with them and give them value, and they'll connect with other people who can benefit your business

Powerful relationships don't just happen from one-time meetings at networking events, you don't need another pocketful of random business cards or Zoom screen-shots to clutter your desk. What you need is a plan to make those connections grow and work for you. And it's not as hard as you think. Here are five essential tactics:

BUILD YOUR NETWORK - IT'S YOUR NEW BUSINESS LIFELINE

Your network includes business colleagues, professional acquaintances, prospective and existing customers, partners, suppliers, contractors and association members, as well as family, friends and people you meet socially and in your community. Contacts have potential customers who are waiting for you to connect with their needs. How do you turn a network of contacts into customers? **Not by hoping they'll remember meeting you six months ago** at a networking event. Networking is a long-term investment.

Do it right by adding value to the relationship, and the contact you just made can really pay off. Communicate like the life of your business depends on it!

COMMUNICATION IS A CONTACT SPORT, SO DO IT EARLY AND OFTEN

No matter how charming, enthusiastic or persuasive you are, no one will likely remember you from a business card or a one-time Zoom meeting. One of the biggest mistakes people make is when they come home or log off from networking events and they fail to follow up. Make the connection immediately. Send a, 'Nice to meet you' email or connect on social media. Immediately, reinforce who you are, what you do and the connection you've made.

You rarely meet people at the exact moment they need what you offe . When they're ready, they will only think of you if you stay on their minds. It's easier to keep a connection warm than to warm it up again once the trail goes cold. So take the time to turn your network of connections into educated customers.

SHARING SUCCESS KEEPS RELATIONSHIPS STRONG

Build your reputation as an expert by giving away what you know. You have interesting things to say! An easy way to communicate is with a brief email (with their permission) that shows prospects why they should buy from you.

Share your wisdom on social media, give advice to entice consumers and leave them wanting more. Contacts and customers who find what you do interesting or valuable will forward and share your message, just like word-of-mouth marketing.

REWARD LOYAL CUSTOMERS, AND THEY'LL REWARD YOU

According to global management consulting firm Bain and Co., a 5% increase in retention yields profit increases of 25 to 100%. And on average, repeat customers spend 67% more than new customers. So your most profitable customers are repeat customers. Are you doing enough to encourage them to work with you again? Stay in touch and give them something of value in exchange for their time, attention and business. It doesn't need to be too much; a personal value-add, invitation to a special event, helpful insights and advice, or news they can use. **Just remember: If you don't keep in touch with your customers, your competitors will.**

LOYAL CUSTOMERS ARE YOUR BEST SALESPEOPLE

Spend the time building your network and do the follow-up. Today, there are cost-effective tools that make this easy. You can email a simple newsletter, an offer or an update message of interest to your network (make sure it's of interest to them, not just to you). Then they'll remember you and what you do and deliver value back to you with referrals. They'll hear about opportunities you'll never hear about. The only way they can say, "Wow, I met somebody who's really good at XYZ. You should give them a call," is if they remember you. Then your customers become your sales force.

If our home is all about location, location, location, then small **business is all about relationships, relationships, relationships**. Find them, nurture them, and watch your sales soar.

See also
The Reality Of Referrals In Business (p135)
What Is Customer Service Really? (p171)
Know, Like, Trust - What Does It Really Mean? (p193)

It's Not The Ingredients, It's What You Do With Them

What have a cake, golf, fishing, a fitness program and a business got in common?

Well, the common factor is the temptation to go out and get the best ingredients, whether flou , eggs and butter, or the most expensive golf clubs you can find, plus strange trousers... a carbon fibre fishing pole, joining the best local gym or having a great business idea and the passion to take it forward.

I spent the early part of my career in the hospitality industry and one key thing I learned is that success comes from the way ingredients are combined, crafted and shaped over time.

I make an awesome cake and it's not because I have the best ingredients, it's because I know how to combine them.

In terms of business, we may well have an amazing product or service, we may have the passion and drive to succeed, but if we don't measure, mix and bake these ingredients correctly, we could end up with just a sticky mess.

Why is it that if we want to bake an amazing cake, we are quite happy to follow a recipe. If we want to get fit, we'll join a gym and take the instruction of a coach.

Yet as soon as we start a business, we say, "It's a learning process and I will have to make my own mistakes."

If I had spent five years making rubbish cakes, I would definitely have been out of a job

I sometimes wonder why so many think the title of 'business owner' automatically brings the title of 'business expert?' Do you think this could be a reason why over 60% of businesses fail in their first five year

See also
Why Start-Ups Sometime Fail (p57)
Getting The Business Basics Right - 8 Tips For Success (p61)
How To Unlock The Power Of Focus (p85)
What Are Big Goals And What Are Ordinary Goals? (p129)

How To Keep Your Battery Charged

We all live our lives at 100 miles an hour, so how can we keep our battery charged with such a demand on our energy.

Our day begins, I hope, with a fully charged battery and, in the same way as a mobile phone uses its battery to run, so do we. As I am working through my day with clients, phone calls, conversations, meetings etc, each part of every conversation uses part of my internal battery charge.

WHAT HAPPENS IF YOUR BATTERY IS NOT FULLY CHARGED EACH DAY

You know the answer, your battery will not last as long. Exactly the same as for your mobile phone. The amount of time and energy you have to invest in the activities in your day is decreased. This is why it is so important to look after yourself. Rather than plug yourself in, take a little time for yourself to recharge your batteries. Make sure you eat well and make sure your health and wellness are catered for. Get enough sleep so your battery can be fully recharged every day.

As a business owner, **I personally am very mindful that my energy levels can decrease over the day** and I am often at my best in the mornings when my battery is fully charged. One of the most important lessons I have learned is to always keep a little bit in reserve so when you are running on low energy, there is still enough power to deliver your best service.

Top tip: never plan your day or week in such a way that your battery is empty every day.

An empty battery always takes longer to recharge than one which still has some energy remaining. If you work in exactly the same way and if you are so busy every day that your battery is exhausted at the end of the day, you will always need to spend more and more time recharging.

WE ARE HYBRIDS

Here is one way I keep my battery charged. In the same way as hybrid batteries in cars, I have learned that I can be of best service to the people I work with by keeping my battery charged. On a daily basis, **I make sure some of the conversations and engagements I have use my energy and some of them recharge my energy.**

This way, I am never on empty at the end of the day.

A very simple tip to look after yourself, your health, your wellness and your ability to support your team and service your clients in the best way you can - think about yourself as having your own internal hybrid battery, like a car. What does it take to keep your battery charged and recharged throughout your day rather than engaging in activities that constantly drain you.

What if your days ended with a full charge rather than what many of us do - end the day tired, exhausted and drained and looking forward to the weekend.

YOUR BATTERY HAS 3 PARTS

I hope you connect with the analogy I'm using, let's take it a step further and propose that your battery has 3 parts.

1. **Your physical battery** - you keep this charged by looking after your physical self with healthy eating, exercise and sufficient rest and down-tim

2. **Your emotional battery** - you keep this charged by spending time with family, friends and loved ones,

and spending time with socially uplifting groups. You can also link physical and emotional with reflective xercise, for example, yoga.

3. **Your intellectual battery** - you keep this charged with self-development and learning, and spending time with people that inspire and support you to improve yourself. I've also learned that my intellectual battery recharges faster with others than it does with individual self-development.

I am very mindful that it is my intellectual battery which is used most professionally, so it's vital that I keep this charged to provide the best service I can at all times. I do this by ensuring my diary includes meetings and conversations with people who inspire me, for example, my own professional mentor.

Whilst you may be good at looking after yourself in most areas, remember that forgetting to look after one part will diminish the effectiveness of the whole.

Look after your battery, keep it charged and keep topping up it up during the day with activities and conversations which inspire, challenge and excite you.

If you would like a conversation about including activities which recharge you everyday, being the best you can all day, drop me a message at mark@mark-jarvis.co.uk.

See also
Be, Do, Have - What Does It Mean? (p107)
Possibilities and Probabilities (p133)
The 60:20:20 Rule (From The Jarvis Principles) (p197)

Invest Money In Your Future

This may seem fairly obvious, nonetheless, by investing money in your future it will:

1. Keep you focused on what you do best.
2. Bring your vision into focus, and
3. Free up time and energy to work on yourself and your business.

When your business starts making money, you need to invest in it - so it continues to grow, thrive and be ever more profitable

Your reinvestment should be in line with your current strategy, aims, vision and plans, this can be for business improvements, marketing or your team, and most importantly, to invest in your own development.

I am consistently amazed (or should I say dismayed) that so many people are willing to invest in their situation here and now but not in their future...

The Ultimate Guide, Or How To Build A Better Business

I've lost count of how many "How to..." guides there about starting and growing businesses.

I think all can be valuable and all have a perspective to offer which may just be the one whch resonates with you.

I believe whatever you decide to do, consistently investing in yourself will ultimately bring what you are working towards.

Here are two of my favourite relevant sayings:

"You will never out-earn your learning".

"It doesn't matter what you want unless you know who you are".

Here's my perspective on what it takes to build a better business:

1. Decide who you are and what values you will live by.
2. Decide why you do what you do (what drives you forward each day).
3. Decide what you want (where do you want to be when your business is done).
4. Build a network of trusted partners (business is a team sport).
5. Work with others who you can help and who can help you.
6. Don't do more - invest in better.

Better means doing those things in order not jumping or missing steps.

It's all too easy to have a good idea and go to market with it without knowing why.

What if the story of Jack and the Beanstalk started with "Jack went to market to try and sell his cow" if we didn't know why?...

See also
How To Avoid The Catch When Finding Your Purpose (p11)
Why Start-Ups Sometimes Fail (p57)
Getting The Business Basics Right - 8 Tips For Success (p61)
Make It Better Before Trying To Make It Bigger (p103)
Which Question I Am Asked Most Often (p209)

Know, Like, Trust - What Does It Really Mean?

But wait, there's more to Know, Like and Trust than you may think. These are terms we use every day in business, perhaps more so for those around me because the people I work with understand they form the foundation of consistent and quality business growth.

Do we really understand what these words mean and the implications they bring?

Here's what I believe to be the real meaning of Know, Like and Trust.

Know - I know you and **why you do what you do**, and you know the same about me.

If you don't truly know why you do what you do, people won't buy from you because people need to know who you are before they buy what you do. Just knowing you and what you do is not enough.

Like - I like you and you like me **because we are alike**. We have shared values, we have similar beliefs and our moral compass is aligned. They say we are the sum of those we surround ourselves with. Having people around us whot are like us means we have no need to try and be something we are not. **Like means like-minded, not just like-able.**

Trust - I trust you and you trust me, but it's not this simple. **Trust is both explicit and implied** and unless we fulfil both, true trust cannot exist. Trust is doing what we say we will do when we say we will do it, promises are kept (explicit) and we live up to the expectations of others (implied). Trust is like a game of Snakes and Ladders where the snakes are always longer than the ladders - go and find your old board game and you will see it's true

For most, we always do what we promise, where some fall down is **they miss the importance of implied promises.**

LET'S SAY A LITTLE MORE ABOUT IMPLIED PROMISES

How often have you had that niggly feeling of being let down by someone whose behaviour didn't quite meet your expectations. Perhaps it was their turn to pay for lunch and they didn't. Perhaps they were late for a meeting and didn't let you know. I know for some, these and other things may seem trivial, but for others, they are important. These hidden expectations we have for others when broken, can mount up and diminish our trust in others. The answer is to clearly communicate both your explicit promises and those more subtle expectations we would ordinarily only share with those very close to us.

Here's another example I think we've all experienced at some point. You've spent time with a prospect or colleague, agreed a follow up only for you to be ignored when you do follow up. Feels awful and frustrating when other do it to us, but think carefully about a time you may have done the same yourself. What makes this example especially relevant is that those who may not be demonstrating behaviour that meets our expectations are the very people who are asking us to trust them!

When we are completely honest with ourselves, I'm sure you will agree that it's not ok to bump an implied promise simply because we believe that fulfilling a cursory demand on our time is more important than fulfilling the implied promises of those we want to trust us. Explicit promises are almost always fulfilled, **don't miss out on the implied** promises you've made if you want those that are like you, to trust you.

BUT WAIT, THERE'S MORE…

Know, **Like** and **Trust** forms the basis of any relationship, whether business or personal.

What if your goal is to generate business, not just more business but better business?

The next step is **Learn** - I have learned from you what a great business opportunity looks like, your target market etc, and you have done the same for me. This is actually a really simple step; **the block happens when people try to share what they are looking for before people trust them**.

In the real world, this often looks like what I call the 'Accidental Referral' where someone says 'do you know anyone who can help me with….' and this opportunity represents itself as a very low risk to reputation. This situation often arises in some types of networking groups. I have found that **people will listen to and act on what you want when they trust you, and not before**.

The final step is **Refer** - Real referrals for better quality business than you are currently getting happen when you have all the above in place and not before.

Most businesses say referrals are an important part of their new client process, why then, since they are so important, are we willing to sit back and wait for them to happen?

Why not develop a strategy that brings you a flow of top-quality referrals?

An active strategy for referrals requires a plan, if you are tired of waiting for referrals to happen for you, now is the time to take action and I'm happy to talk with you about what building a plan in your business could look like.

Know, Like and Trust, even in its simplest form, is wasted energy if you don't do something, and simply sitting back and waiting for it to happen will ultimately lead to disappointment, you need to add the **Learn** and **Refer** steps to create genuine results.

See also
The Reality Of Referrals In Business Today (p135)
Why Aren't You More Profitable In Your Network? (p149)
How Do You Know If Those In Your Network Are The Right People (p159)
Which Came First, The Sales Pipeline Or The Relationship Pipeline? (p167)
The Top Seven Barriers To Referrals (p203)

The 60:20:20 Rule
(From The Jarvis Principles)

I am often asked; How much time I should spend working ON my business and how much time I should spend working IN my business?

Here's a simple model which will help you get an inside track on where I believe you should be in terms of the balance between in your business, on your business and on yourself. Please note, I've also found this principle applies to all, from sole-trader to the leaders of multi-million and multi-national organisations. The busier we get, the less time we focus on development and growth.

This is something I have come up with after many years in business myself starting, growing and selling businesses. The one constant in all I have learned, including the people I have worked with, currently work with, and will work with, is they spend the majority of their time working in their business. **In the early years it is absolutely right we spend the majority of our time working in our business** because working in our business means that we are delivering what the business does, beginning to grow our team and make money.

The trick is in knowing when and how to grow beyond just being busy. For the majority of people what then tends to happen is, as people get busier, they spend a higher and higher percentage of their time working in their business, leaving less and less time to work on their business and even on themselves. In fact, **most people**

sacrifice working on their business and on themselves to work more and more in their business as they get more customers, their team grows, and they get busier. This still rings true even if working on the business is your role. If not now, this tipping point will come to you at some point soon.

I want to share this with you today so you can see it coming, act now and be ready for it. What is the answer?

A very simple model really. **I believe people should be working 60% of their time in their business, 20% of their time on their business, and 20% of their time on themselves.**

When I say time, I mean the total amount of time you assign to work, not the total amount of time in a week.

GEORGE'S SIMPLE EXAMPLE

George has a working week of 40 hours over 5 days. Using my model George would spend 24 hours working in his business, 8 hours working on his business and 8 hours working on himself.

Take a moment to be honest with yourself, are you actually doing this or something like it, or are you just running week to week, month to month hoping your business will grow? Please trust me when I say, your business may get busier, but it will not grow if you have no time for planning and growth activities.

GROWING DOES NOT HAVE TO MEAN BIGGER, BUT IT ALWAYS MEANS BETTER.

Like many preconceptions in business the term 'grow a business' and 'build a bigger business', seem to be intrinsically linked. The reality is growing a business does not have to mean growing a bigger business, but it does always have to mean growing a better and more profitable business. It is absolutely right that some people don't want to expand their business in terms of employing more people, having a bigger offic or more locations. Although more do when they're honest with themselves, they just don't know how. **That does not excuse any of us from our responsibility to grow a better, more profitable business.**

Tipping Point 1; when you find yourself sacrificing working on your business and on yourself time just to service more customers or manage more people more often, you need to grow into different customers and learn about effective delegation

LET'S DIG A LITTLE DEEPER

Let us say that you are now working 60% of your time in your business. What does in your business mean. In your business means the time spent doing what your business or role does, for example delivering your product or service, marketing, sales, HR, finance, social media, admin, networking and **anything related to these tasks are still working in your business**. Unfortunately, so many people I talk with believe marketing, sales, social media, networking, admin, and more management meetings etc, are working on the business activities when they are not.

HOW TO BREAK DOWN WORKING IN YOUR BUSINESS

You are now spending 60% of your time working in your business doing all the things a business does, including delivery, marketing, sales, HR, finance, social media, networking and admin. **My recommendation is to spend 50% of your time in delivering what your business does, and 10% of your time on other business activities** - all the other things a business or your role has to do to operate.

Tipping Point 2; when you find yourself spending more than 10% of your time doing all the other things a business has to do, **it's time to out-source or delegate.**

GEORGE'S CONTINUING STORY

George now has a model which supports growth - remember, growth means better, better you, better business and better future. He is working for 20 hours delivering what his business does, 4 hours in other business activities as described above, 8 hours on his business or role and 8 hours on himself. Sounds good right? **So why are you not doing this or at least working towards this now**.

George now has 8 hours to spend working on his business and a further 8 hours working on himself, what will he do? The simple reality is that **most people do not know what to do with that time**, and neither did George, so he just filled the time with more customers and more management meetings. Not a bad thing you may say, but **where is growth in that strategy**.

What George is doing, and what you could do with 16 hours is beyond the scope of this article. There's a real life example case study on my website where John's financial planning business saved 7 hours per week through efficiencie giving him time to work with his team of 12 on growth and planning.

YOU WILL NEVER OUT EARN YOUR LEARNING

I believe if you are going to grow a successful business or organisation, not only do you need to work on your business, but you also need to work on yourself. Without constantly improving yourself in your business, who you are and how you work, all you can ever expect to be is busy, doing more of the same things you have always done. Of course, if that is all you ever want, then doing more of what you have always done is absolutely fine. What happens when you run out of time though?

I believe as responsible business owners, partners, directors or managers, we have a duty to work towards a better future for us and those we love. The Japanese have a word you may have heard before - Kaizen, which in its shortest form means 'constant improvement', read more about this concept through Google or Wikipedia.

See also
How To Achieve The Second Goal Of Every Business Owner (p1)
How To Unlock The Power Of Focus (p85)
Make It Better Before Trying To Make It Bigger (p103)
How To Solve The Problem Of The Entrepreneurs Second See-Saw (p121)
What Does Making Changes In Business Really Mean? (p163)

Mark Jarvis

The Top Seven Barriers To Consistent Quality Referrals

Today I thought I would share with you what I have found to be the **biggest barriers to consistent quality referrals in business**. It would be very easy to do what most people do and share with you what does work. Lots of things do work, but I have found that there are just a few things which stop referrals - DEAD!

If you are interested in what to avoid, continue reading.

I think we all know what prevents referrals, this bit is easy, here are a couple - not asking, asking too early and not following up. Today I'm sharing with you what stops consistent quality, which I hope you see is somewhat different

Here we go - starting with my number one barrier, bar none, to consistent quality referrals:

1. **Asking before trust is built.** Consistent referrals happen when relationships are formed, just because you participate in a network, don't think all you need to do is ask. Yes, you might get the odd one-off referral, but you won't get consistent quality without relationships and trust.

2. **Asking the wrong people.** Please note, here I am talking about what you want next, not more of what you already get. Quality comes from always aiming for better. This means what you want next may not be available from the people you are currently around.

3. **Not knowing what quality means to you**. A simple answer here - if you don't know what you want, how on earth do you think your network will know!

4. **Not knowing why you want what you want**. At this level, I have found consistent quality referrals come from those who buy into you, why you do what you do and what you are aiming for. Clarity brings consistency.

5. **Not training your network**. As in the above points, consistently sharing with your key people what you are looking for next, will bring you the referrals and business opportunities you want. Please note, next in this case means BETTER not MORE.

6. **Not understanding how to exchange value**. At this elevated level, simply exchanging referrals is not enough. Understanding how to exchange real value in your network is the key to consistent quality.

7. **Trying to 'buy' referrals**. I will simply state here: if you are looking for volume then incentivising your referral sources can work, BUT, if you are looking for consistent quality, I strongly advise you to develop a value-based reward system that is NOT a percentage or monetary system.

I appreciate that my explanations are short, I hope they have at least got you thinking.

Do please check out the other chapters as they go into more detail about what real quality and consistency in referrals actually means.

See also
The Reality Of Referrals In Business (p135)
Why Aren't You More Profitable In Your Network? (p149)
How Do You Know If Those Around You Are The Right People? (p159)
Which Came First, The Sales Pipeline Or The Relationship Pipeline? (p167)
Know, Like And Trust, What Does It Really Mean? (p193)

The Difference Between Word Of Mouth And Referral Marketing

In marketing, there is always a new buzzword which gets marketers excited. Whereas 'word of mouth' was hot a few years ago, we are now hearing a lot about 'referral marketing', particularly with the growth of referral focused networking groups. **If you think that the two are similar, you are right, but they are not the same.** They both involve customers talking about a brand or product, but referral marketing is measurable and repeatable. It can be controlled, focused and targeted. Word of mouth is more about reaction and spontaneity. We really cannot control it.

As business owners, we are (or should be) all about what we can control, right?

REFERRAL MARKETING AS AN END-TO-END SOLUTION

Where businesses might have just dabbled in referral marketing in the past, they are now starting to use it in a more involved and in-depth manner, because it can be tracked. With a fully immersed strategy, referrals become predictable; quality improves as do conversion rates.

Businesses investing in a referral marketing strategy to run alongside their existing sales and marketing programs are discovering what we always knew to be true; **referrals cost less, convert faster and in most cases are more profitable.**

There is a growing understanding that to be fully effective, the opportunity for real quality referrals can no longer just sit as a call to action at the bottom of a website, in a networking elevator pitch, an email footer, or within a customer conversation. It has to be planned for, tracked and given the importance its profitability brings

THE LONG-TERM VALUE OF A REFERRED CUSTOMER

All the bells and whistles of referral marketing are nice, but does it actually work? I have to answer with a resounding yes and here's why. Based on a study by completed in 2011 (yes, over ten years ago, and yet most businesses still do not effectively generate real referrals) the following statistics were given; referred customers are about 25% more profitable per year for businesses than their non-referred counterparts. They are 18% less likely to churn, and they have a 25% higher lifetime value than non-referred customers, even after factoring in any costs.

WHAT ABOUT THAT PESKY ROI?

If there is one buzzword we are all sick of hearing, it is Return on Investment, 'ROI'. Marketers will argue tactics for measuring things like social media hits, likes and engagement into the ground. But how can we track the ROI of referral marketing?

Treating referral marketing as a strategy and a plan means we know exactly what we are spending in both money and time for each quality referral we receive, including the rewards we give to advocates and new customers. In the same way as we know (or should know) the cost of sale in our sales pipeline, we also now know the cost per referral. We can track the lifetime value of a customer through both our traditional sales pipeline and now our referral pipeline.

USING REFERRAL MARKETING TO GAIN REPEAT CUSTOM.

While certainly referral marketing serves to attract new customers, a well-developed strategy can also bring them back and help them refer on. Offering incentives can drive repeat business and whilst opinions on whether this tactic works consistently are divided, there clearly is a place in business for this. After all, some of the largest businesses in the world use this tactic.

My final thoughts - **referral marketing works, but only with a strategy and plan**. The days of simply reacting and waiting are over. If you are serious about the potential power contained within a quality driven referral marketing strategy, then take action today.

See also
The Reality Of Referrals In Business (p135)
Which Came First, The Sales Pipeline Or The Relationship Pipeline? (p167)
The Top Seven Barriers To Consistent Quality Referrals (p203)

A Lesson In Networking

Here's a tip that will help you build a stronger network.

Imagine you are hosting a party and you are thinking about your guest list, who will you invite and who will you strategically 'forget' to invite?

You will invite those you know and like and not those you don't like.

Building a trusted network is exactly the same - who will you invite to join your network and who will you miss out? Generally, we start by believing that more people in our network is better. **I've learned that more is not better simply because we have to factor in trust.** When trust is a factor, it becomes vital to have the right people around us.

Now imagine your network is all in one room, however big that room might be.

Now imagine the door to the room only goes one way. Whoever you let in, is in forever.

I'm sure you agree that getting the right people in your room is more important than having more people in your room.

Building trust is simple (not easy), do what you say you will do when you say you will do it and don't ever let that slip, ever!

Which Question I Am Asked Most Often

Of all the questions I am asked on a regular basis, including 'How do I find the right people for my team?' and 'How do I get better customers?', by a long way, the question I am asked most often is: 'How do I grow my business?'

The answer to that question is, I believe, actually very simple, so I guess you want to know…

But, before we get to it, let me just be clear and say, this is the answer, not the solution.

Results and outcomes are created when a series of actions are implemented over time when the right people have the right information, and they are willing to act.

Of course, this is entirely individual. It seems strange to me that so many see getting an answer as a solution! A good example of this belief would be the huge number of workshops and webinars that continually pop up. Our temptation is to get lots of answers only to find that the answer doesn't bring results. **All the best workshop and webinar hosts will tell you it is not what you learn today, but what you put into action forever which truly makes the difference.**

WHAT'S THE ANSWER?

The answer to the 'ultimate business question', as any *Hitchhikers Guide To The Galaxy* fan might tell you, is not in fact 42, however temptingly attractive this simple answer may be.

I believe the answer has three steps and I have found these three steps in almost every business as it grows and scales.

1. Work hard and overcome all the challenges and hurdles that life and business throw at you and hope it will be alright in the end. Whilst this may work, it will take all your time, money and energy until you either deliberately or accidentally hit on the solution.

2. Do something different with what you already know. Again, this may work eventually. The reality is many people convince themselves that doing the same things they have always done, even if in a different way, is a step towards a solution. Because you are still doing all the same things, you still often only stumble across the solution.

3. Surround yourself with people who have already achieved what you want to achieve and learn from them. From learning from your parents to your years in formal education, the real power of learning comes from others. Surrounding yourself with those who have the success you desire, and learning from them, is the best way to answer the question "How do I grow my business."

The question now becomes; How long are you willing to wait and how many times are you willing to try different things? Perhaps you are willing to try five different things, perhaps ten?

Perhaps you are willing to wait one year, two years, five years, or more, before seeing the success you desire.

My challenge to all of you as owners, partners and directors of businesses, no matter the size or age: **Do something today that means you are not trying, hoping or**

wishing, but actually doing and achieving. That success only comes from learning from others. Who will you be learning from and who will you teach?

See also
Why Creative Distraction Is Holding You Back (p65)
How To Unlock The Power Of Focus (p85)
What Does Making Changes In Business Really Mean? (p163)

Mark Jarvis

Meaningful Goals

Seems everyone starts talking about goal setting at the beginning of the year. Rather than do what most do and talk about the importance of setting goals, I will simply share this:

You will always fail to hit a goal you are not aiming at.

I think you get it... Now that's out of the way, let's talk about what will make a difference for you. Setting goals and planning to achieve them is vital if you are going to see the future you want.

But what goals do you set? It's too easy to set goals which describe more turnover, bigger team and faster growth when what underlies these goals can be so much more powerful.

Here are some ideas to get you started.

1. Set a goal for how much time you want to get back each quarter. Now you can focus on the right activities to get you there. Why? Because being as busy as you are today is unsustainable and not what you signed up for.

2. Set a goal for how much you want to increase your profitabilit , not just turnover. What's the point of doubling your turnover if your net profit decreases?

3. Set a goal for personal and team performance and productivity. Plan to invest in yourself and your team, recruitment, retention and wellbeing.

Reviewing your numbers this year and simply adding a few zero's to next year's goals won't cut it if you are truly committed to scaling your business.

See also
How To Unlock The Power Of Focus (p85)
Is Today Your Last Groundhog Day? (p117)
What Are Big Goals And What Are Ordinary Goals? (p129)
Why Running A Business Should Be Like Driving A Car (p217)

The Perpetual Motion Business

As far back as the 1400s scientists and inventors have been trying to create a machine which runs forever without requiring any further input and energy. **The concept of perpetual motion has been something we have sought for hundreds of years** and there are many stories around the concept of the everlasting battery from the *Mission Impossible* film series, or the everlasting gobstopper from *Charlie and the Chocolate Factory*.

The concept of a machine or product that lasts forever is clearly a very attractive proposition, and certainly it would be wonderful if we could invent an engine which required no fuel. Despite many attempts over hundreds of years, the perpetual motion machine continues to be an impossible dream, not least because it would break the laws of physics!

The concept of a perpetual motion machine got me thinking about how this might apply to us in business. I have always been led to believe that the goal of a business owner is to create a business to run by itself, or to create a business which doesn't require them to be there. This feels like a direct analogy with the concept of a perpetual motion machine which runs with no further input, very much like the traditional aim to build a perpetual motion business.

In the same way as a perpetual motion machine is beyond our reach, so is a perpetual motion business.

Whilst we can work hard to create and build our business, it cannot run without the further investment of fuel or energy to keep it running. There just must be some level of energy invested in the system to keep the system running.

Creating a perpetual motion business is theoretically and practically impossible. Building an efficien business is possible and does not require an awful lot of investment but does require the right type of investment.

I have found investing in the right fuel and energy in business can yield amazing results.

Start with disciplined people, give them the responsibility to succeed and the knowledge to implement and we can all build an efficien business. Anything less will mean we have to invest a disproportionate amount of time and energy to keep it growing.

Whilst we can't create a perpetual motion business machine, we can create a very efficien business by engaging with highly disciplined and driven people, giving them the responsibility and inspiration to succeed, then fuelling them with new and relevant information.

Whether we have an established business with a leadership and management structure or a small business with one or two staff; who we have around us - our team, customers and network, will dictate the efficiency of our busines

See also
How To Achieve The Second Goal Of Every Business Owner (p1)
How To Get Recruitment Right First Time - Part 1 (p19)
How To Get Recruitment Right First Time - Part 2 (p25)
How To Avoid Random Acts Of Delegation (p45)
What Does Packard's Law Teach Us About Business Growth? (p223)

Why Running A Business Should Be Like Driving A Car

Driving a car requires all sorts of skills and learning and I believe the principles of running a business and driving a car are very similar, and here's why. Imagine yourself sitting in the driving seat of your car, thinking about the journey. Perhaps you know where you are going and how to get there, or perhaps you plug in the satnav.

As you begin to drive along, you check the rear-view and side mirrors, you look and listen to what's around you and you listen to the sounds the car is making. You are aware of what's behind you, other vehicles that may be approaching, but, **most of your time is spent looking ahead**, looking for the next bend in the road, junction, roundabout or obstacle, perhaps even another car to overtake.

I believe running a business should be like driving a car because you should spend the same amount of time looking ahead in your businesses as you do looking ahead when driving.

In reality, too many business owners spend most of their time looking at what's behind them, focusing on what's around them, their short-term goals (out of the side window), and not enough time looking and planning for what's ahead. Trust me when I say that if you don't look far enough ahead, you are going to crash, maybe not now, but soon.

Like driving, **the further ahead you look, the better you can plan** and be prepared for your journey. If you use a satnav, you are given clear guidance on what's ahead so you can take appropriate action and not take a wrong turn.

Like a car, your business must be maintained, serviced and upgraded. It's not enough to just go out and buy a car (start a business), put fuel in it (get customers), and expect the car to run forever, it won't, so you must invest.

DO YOU SEE YOUR CAR AS A COST OR AN INVESTMENT?

Like a car, your business is there as a platform to move your life from where you are to where you want to be.

Next time you are out driving, or even a passenger, be aware of how much of the time you are looking ahead and focussing on where you are going not where you have been, and how much time you are planning for your arrival.

Now work on applying the same principles in your business, look further ahead than you are now, be better prepared and if you are not sure how to get there, use the best satnav you can find. In business, the best satnav would be a mentor or coach.

I hope this analogy has resonated with you and I hope it helps you think about looking ahead rather than behind or to the side.

I'll leave you with one final thought - what will you do if your competition is a better driver than you, or they have a better car and you haven't invested in your own skills as a driver, or invested in maintaining and improving your car?

See also
What Makes A Great Footballer? (p173)
The 60:20:20 Rule (From The Jarvis Principles) (p197)
The Perpetual Motion Business (p215)

What's The Difference Between A Teacher, A Coach, And A Mentor?

You can't add value if you don't have anything of value to add.

I believe it's rare for anyone to find success without having one or more people around them to help, support and guide them on life's journey, and this is as true in business as it is personally.

I'll challenge you to name one sports personality, pop star or celebrity who hasn't had some sort of coaching or support. **Why then, do we, as business-people expect success without help and see getting the right help as optional?**

When asked, I often describe myself as a teacher first, a mentor second and a coach third. And this is why. When I first started my journey in business, I didn't know what to do so what I needed first was a teacher. As I continued my journey in business, I needed a mentor to show me how to implement what I'd learned and only then did I need someone to keep me on track and coach me as I grew and my business scaled.

Many people in business don't actually know what to do to take themselves and their business to the next level, beyond what is in the here and now. The first step therefore has to be make sure you are ready to take action, then learn what to do, then how to do it. It doesn't matter how big or small your business is, whether you are established or new, or what role you have within a business, every time you are ready to take the next step, the process is the same. **Get ready to act, learn what to do and invest in implementation over time to achieve the results you desire.**

When you consider who to engage to help you, perhaps you should ask yourself if what you actually need is knowledge and implementation first. In our modern world, knowledge and information is free, we all have access to the same information anytime we want it. Why then do so many still struggle with the same challenges in business as they have always faced. **Knowing what to do to fix my car doesn't make me a mechanic, and attending a social media workshop won't suddenly revolutionise my business.**

Knowing what to do is no longer enough, if it was, we would all live in a mansion and drive a Ferrari. Knowing how to take action and implement what you learn is where the secret to success lies. No successful sports person ever became so by going on a course or reading the latest book, they became successful by practicing over time with the help and guidance of a mentor or coach. It's all a matter of priorities.

Quick wins in the here and now are all very well but long-term success is simply not possible without help. What kind of help is most important to you?

1. A great teacher needs people who are keen to learn, has something worthwhile teaching, retains respect for those learning and the ability to listen more than to talk.

2. A coach does not need business experience, just the ability to bring out the best from the people they work with.

3. A mentor has experience in business with knowledge, skills and techniques to share that the recipient does not yet have.

Think about what sort of help is right for you now and in the future so you can move forward, grow and scale your business with confidence, and achieve the goals you decided upon when you began your journey. For me it was because I wanted to own my own journey and decide when and for whom I would work. It took me a long time to realise I was just going through the motions and being busy. Simply because I didn't get the help I needed soon enough. Don't let this be you, too!

"You can't add value if you don't have anything of value to add"

See also
How To Unlock The Power Of Focus (p85)
Be, Do, Have - What Does It Mean? (p107)
Is Today Your Last Groundhog Day? (p117)
What Are Big Goals And What Are Ordinary Goals? (p129)

Mark Jarvis

What Does Packard's Law Teach Us About Business Growth?

Picture this - You are in a company that is growing fast. You might even be the CEO. You are consumed by designing a great product or service, getting it built, and figuring out how best to sell it. You have hit everyone's social network every month for a year to hire your hard-working employees. You have even paid several recruiting agencies, but you cannot hire fast enough to keep up with market forces and growing demand. You are now entering the world defined by Packard's Law (of Hewlett Packard fame).

PACKARD'S LAW

"No company can grow revenues consistently faster than its ability to get enough of the right people to implement that growth and still become a great company."

If your growth rate in revenues consistently outpaces your growth rate in people, you simply will not - indeed cannot - build a great company." **David Packard**.

Packard's Law should be one of just a few irrefutable laws that shape business growth as the message is clear for all to see - you cannot grow your business outside the quality of your people. The key message being the 'right people', not 'any people' who you then try to shape into 'your people'.

I am reminded of the movie *Captain America* - the story, for those who haven't seen it, even though you will have seen the story played out many times. Take an average looking individual with limited skills and turn him into an all-conquering hero. What's the differentiato ; attitude and integrity - the right person.

Steve Jobs often said, "Make sure you're hiring only A⁺ players." Hire a few B players, he said, and they hire B's and C's, and pretty soon the whole operation is going to pot. Steve also said, "A small team of A⁺ players can run circles around a giant team of B and C players."

To guarantee growth in your business, get the right people in the right places in your organisation, only then give them the skills to deliver in their role.

Using Steve Jobs' philosophy, if you want to build a thriving and successful business that is growing, get A⁺ people around you. To do that, you must be an A⁺ person first yoursel .

Being an A⁺ person is not about knowledge and skill, it's not about being an expert in every area of business, it's all about attitude and integrity (*Captain America*). **If you don't have these first, you cannot invent it or hire it.**

Packard's Law may seem erroneous or irrelevant, especially if you are a solopreneur or micro business, however, no matter your role, position or responsibility, the size or age of your business, **when you start with the right people who have the right attitude, growth becomes inevitable rather than aspirational**, and that applies as much to your network and your customers and suppliers as it does to yourself.

See also
How To Get Recruitment Right First Time - Part 1 (p19)
How To Get Recruitment Right First Time - Part 2 (p25)
The Secret To Cultural Success In Business (p71)
The Key To Organisational Health (p93)
Five Top Tips For Managing A Growing Team (p229)

Time Limited Turnover - The Eternal Business Challenge

Time limited turnover is a phenomenon familiar to all of us who have ever started a business, grown a business, or worked in a business.

The number one symptom is busy-ness. It's true, we all get busy doing the things we do - from working with clients and customers, networking, sales and admin, to managing and leading our staff and team

The challenge is simply this: when presented with an opportunity or desire to grow, a requirement for investment is created, yet we are unable to invest because we have no time left in our busy schedule to increase our turnover or capacity to match.

More and more people expand their expenditure to match their income. Many do this in their personal life so why not in business?

In your personal life you set aside an amount each month for savings and your retirement fund to secure your future, your business should be the same.

GROWTH IS A RESULT OF INVESTMENT NOT COST CUTTING

If you are truly serious about growing yourself and your business, your organisation, your team, and building a better future, investment must be your top priority.

When your priority is customers, clients, or anything other than investment, you have no choice but to be busier, and yes, your turnover may increase, but one day, perhaps even now, your capacity for turnover will be capped by your available time. Sadly, for many at this point, it can be too late.

You are spending all your income, you are as busy as you can be, yet when you want to grow, you cannot because you have no spare cash to invest and you cannot be any busier to earn it.

Many often resort to cost-cutting and 'trying to do it themselves', and then begins the slippery slope… What I will say is that in business, there is a solution for busy-ness.

In the same way as you do in your personal life, set aside an amount to secure your business future. My recommendation, between 5% and 10% of your monthly turnover. I use a percentage because as your business, organisation and team grows, you need to increase your investment levels.

Look at it this way, imagine you plant a beautiful flower in your garden - would you save costs by never watering it, would you save time by never tending to it - of course not. Why? Because it will not grow and thrive and in many cases it may die.

Whatever your business, organisation, position or role, your capacity is limited by your time. **Unless you invest, growth can be nothing more than accidental.**

Being busy is not a measure of success at any level. **Being busy forever is neither desirable or sustainable, it's not what you signed up for, being increasingly profitable is.**

Please do not get caught up in this concept of Time Limited Turnover, almost every business I know has or will unless they take action and get help from those that have lived this journey and who's businesses are thriving not just surviving.

See also
How To Get Recruitment Right First Time - Part 1 (p19)
How To Get Recruitment Right First Time - Part 2 (p25)
Getting The Business Basics Right (p61)
Make It Better Before Trying To Make It Bigger (p103)
How To Solve The Problem Of The Entrepreneurs Second See-Saw (p121)
What Does Making Changes In Business Really Mean? (p163)
The 60:20:20 Rule (From The Jarvis Principles) (p197)

Mark Jarvis

Five Top Tips For Managing A Growing Team

The ones who think they are crazy enough to change the world are the ones who do.

Growth, it's what every successful business strives to achieve year on year. From turnover and profit, to products and services, we all work to targets to keep our business profitable and thriving. Inevitably, as your business grows and scales, so will your team.

A growing team can bring new and exciting opportunities for a business. From years of relevant experience to fresh ideas, new team members can help to push your business in the right direction and inject energy into an established team. HOWEVER, new team members also mean change, and change for many, particularly in the workplace, can be a challenge.

HOW WILL A NEW TEAM MEMBER AFFECT YOUR CURRENT TEAM?

The current team have ways of working efficiently with one another, they know their role inside out, know each other's quirks, the systems used and protocols followed, and the workarounds and flexibility needed regularly.

With that in mind, how can you effectively grow your team and make significant changes without creating conflict and challenge?

Here are my five top tips to ensure harmony in a growing team:

COMMUNICATION IS KEY

Vulnerability and uncertainty are two areas common in teams that are growing, and whilst direction and process can't necessarily fix this, effective communication ca

Effectively communicating changes before, during, and after can help remove the uncertainty felt through any growth transitions.

Ideally, everyone should be working from the same knowledge base. By this, I mean encouraging collaboration. Making your current team part of the process can help those challenged, feel less vulnerable. Using 'open book' leadership and management strategies and being transparent will ensure your team understand why new members are joining, what they can bring to the business, and everyone's part in new and collaborative targets.

Ask your team how these changes impact them, ask them to offer suggestions for positive change, ensure you have regular 'brainstorming' meetings. When you effectively manage the process through clear communication you can see issues coming before they become a full-on challenge.

ENSURE SUITABLE, EFFECTIVE AND EFFICIENT SYSTEMS ARE IN PLACE

I have already alluded to the likelihood that your team is comfortable with your current systems and processes. Before you train a new team member, check whether what you have now, is still fit for purpose. With an expanding team, there is a good chance that you may quickly outgrow your current systems (which could be as simple as using shared documents and online resources). If you are used to a team of two or three, injecting a couple more people can mean workloads suddenly become overwhelming and confusing, and this is when friction increases.

A growing team is usually a result of a growing business. It provides the perfect time to introduce a new project management tool, new systems and processes to keep workloads and team members organised, collaborative and efficient It also allows you, as the leader and manager, to keep an overview of everyone's workload, delegate tasks, prioritise jobs and ensure your team is working efficient .

Teamwork, Monday.com, Asana, and Hubspot are all software tools that can keep your team on a collaborative and efficient trac

APPRECIATE YOUR CURRENT TEAM

A growing team usually results from a thriving business. Your current team members are doing such an excellent job that the business is growing, and therefore you need to add extra resources, which includes further additions to the team.

When change occurs, your team may feel vulnerable and insecure. Workloads increase, new systems are introduced, and all their excellent work can be taken for granted, especially when you are focussed on a new team member or you ask your current team to train a new team member, and where additional tasks are being added to their to-do list.

I have already talked about clear communication and inclusion, and appreciation should closely follow. Be sure to recognise, thank, praise and reward team members for their efforts. When someone is doing a great job, a simple personal message of thanks can make a huge difference to wellbeing and a feeling of being valuable - even better, a small gift, perhaps treating the team to lunch on a Friday to say thank you.

When team members actively receive praise and acknowledgment, this can inspire collaboration and team spirit, which is precisely what is needed during times of change.

Keep recognition consistent and straightforward and, where possible, in line with your organisational and cultural values and vision.

ESTABLISH A CLEAR CORPORATE CULTURE

Speaking of culture, consistently communicating the organisation's culture, values, vision and beliefs, can really inspire team collaboration. Effective communication establishes a clear corporate culture within your team, ensures they are clear on the company's vision and mission and understand where the business is heading and how it intends to get there.

When new team members join, be sure to onboard them with the company's culture at the forefront of their induction, consistency is key to a strong team. Part of a collaborative culture would include you organising regular team activities outside of work, and your training and development plan being at the forefront of growth. Put in place personal development plans with your team to encourage individual and group training and career development and ensure you are constantly and consistently delivering your vision.

MANAGE CONFLICT

In an ideal world, we are liked by all, and we enjoy the company of everyone we meet. In reality, conflict happens, whether personally or through workplace pressure. Conflict at work is not uncommon and a key symptom can be personal fulfilment and motivation, or lack of it. Your team will likely come from diverse backgrounds, they will have varying opinions and beliefs, they will have different personalities and will have worked in different businesses with different cultures

Conflict can lead to hostility and resentment very quickly unless managed effectively.

The theme emerging from this article is communication, inclusion and reward. Managing conflict in the workplace can be reduced by allowing everyone a voice to share their concerns. There are many other symptoms of conflict, too many to detail here. I have found there can be underlying feelings of resentment within organisations the managers and leaders are unaware of, so make sure you check in with your team regularly.

IN A NUTSHELL

Growing your team means change, and change requires effective and proactive leadership and management in all you do and deliver through your team.

Lead by example, keep abreast of any issues that may arise, involve your team (both new and existing) in the process, communicate regularly throughout and you won't go far wrong.

See also
How To Avoid Random Acts Of Delegation (p45)
The Key To Cultural Success In Business (p71)
The Key To Organisational Health (p93)
The Five Most Important Things To Do When Creating A Team Skills Development Plan (p99)
Make It Better Before Trying To Make It Bigger (p103)
Why People Leave People (p111)
What Does Making Changes In Business Really Mean? (p163)

What Makes A Great Leader

The direction in which a leader looks helps to identify whether they are a good leader or a great one.
1. Great leaders look in the mirror not out of the window when apportioning responsibility.
2. Great leaders look in the mirror not out of the window when apportioning blame.
3. Great leaders look out of the window not in the mirror when apportioning credit.
4. Great leaders look out of the window not in the mirror when apportioning power.

Whether you are a worker, a supervisor, a manager, or a director, you may even have a leadership title now, developing your leadership skills means living by these four points.

Before you dismiss these points because you think you are not a leader, consider this.

Someone, somewhere thinks you are.

Are You Working In Transaction World Or Relationship World?

In transaction world, currency is money. In relationship world your currency is trust.

Trust is the only currency that matters, here's why.

Trust and money are so intrinsically linked that:

- You can get more, you can get less.
- You have to earn both.
- Both can appreciate in value when you invest, and depreciate when you don't.
- Both are exchanged between customers, suppliers and your team.

Here is an interesting idea; how does the concept of 'interest' affect both

I think it's pretty easy to see how interest rates affect money. When rates are high, you earn more from your savings and borrowing costs you more. When rates are low, you earn less from your savings and borrowing costs you less.

How about the interest rate for trust. I believe the interest rate for trust can be defined as **how much self-interest you have in a relationship.**

If either party has a high degree of self-interest, then trust tends to be low because it's clear to one another that some other expectation is on the table and trust is reduced.

Think about that for a minute if you have a financial incentive based referral system in your business.

Here's a typical example; you meet someone for the first or even second time and assuming they don't immediately try to sell to you, which thankfully seems to happen less often that it used to, you start talking about how you can help each other, what sort of business each of you are looking for, and you agree notionally to 'keep an eye out' for opportunities for each other. **The problem here is that both parties are more interested in what they can gain rather than what they can give** - self-interest is high making trust low. You can find this phenomenon in referral-based networking groups, especially with newer members.

Here's the key difference - **if you have trust, money doesn't matter, if you don't have trust, money is the only thing that matters**. Think about this concept in your sales process.

Why do you think so many businesses try to sell their stuff using money as leverage - because they have not invested in trust. Special offers, free stuff, price beating/matching are perfect examples of this, as is the fear of increasing prices above your competition.

I think we can all see that living in transaction world means those who do are always chasing quantity over quality, and quantity is finite whereas quality can always be improved upon.

If you want to grow a strong, sustainable business then invest in trust and live in a relationship world, if you just want money, work hard and hope the interest rate doesn't bite you.

See also
What Trust Should Be (p131)
Which Came First, The Sales Pipeline Or The Relationship Pipeline? (p167)
Know, Like, Trust - What Does It Really Mean? (p193)

How Much Does It Cost To Hire A Business Coach?

When thinking about getting help, most people have three burning questions:
1. I have done ok so far, why would I need any help?
2. How long will it take?
3. How much will it cost?

If you don't think you need or want any help, you are either way ahead in your goals, or you're stuck and can't admit it. How long it will take depends entirely on how far you want to go. For example, do you just need support through a project or significant change, or are you working towards exit years ahead.

This chapter is mainly focussed on question 3; How much will it cost?

If you are thinking of working with a business coach or mentor, your main question is probably 'How much?' and quite rightly for some, a major concern.

You will want to know what you get for the investment, whether they charge by the hour or have a fixed fee, a choice of fixed programmes and of course, whether they offer any guarantee of success

As you may have already seen, there are many different pricing options out there, and they vary widely depending on who you use. So let's have a look at some of these options and which one best fits what YOU want and need.

Next time you go to the supermarket to buy bread, see how many options there are. You can buy a brand or a style. You can buy on size and the number of slices, you can buy fresh and slice yourself, and you can buy on longevity and sustainability. This list goes on. Most of the time, you probably buy what you like. **So do remember working with someone you like and respect may be more valuable than simply price.**

FRANCHISED VS INDEPENDENT

There are a number of coaching franchises available, eg. ActionCoach, Entrepreneurs Operating System, Business Doctors and The Entrepreneurs Circle to name a few. There are more of course, and all bring value. It's not my place to give an opinion, I will simply state, a franchised coach will have to pay franchise fees which inevitably means that all are likely to have a higher starting price than independent coaches who work for themselves and manage their own fees.

A franchise coach will often work with repeating programmes (see Point 2) and may use tried and tested systems to help you grow your business. Their prices typically range from £500 to £2000 per month over a fixed term or contract.

Whilst there may be a minimum level or experience required to take on a coaching franchise, there is nothing to stop almost anyone buying a franchise or going on a course, and setting themselves up as a business coach.

Independent coaches will be more flexible in their approach and their pricing.

They will have built their business or businesses themselves and should have the work/life balance that you aspire to. Prices can vary immensely, typically from £100 on a session by session basis, through to £1000+. Most will be somewhere in the middle.

Business coaching and mentoring is an unregulated industry so you will often find coaches talking about their qualifications, achievements and accolades but are they truly getting the results their clients want. **It is therefore vital that you understand what you want, and any good mentor/coach should help you with this right from the start.** Think about the kind of results you want, and how much it would be worth to you. We all understand that we get what we pay for so please don't expect a 5-star service from a 3-star investment.

You will find those with a huge amount of experience in the corporate world, involved in or running huge multi-nationals, but how relevant is this to you in your micro or small business. Personally, I choose to work with those with relevant experience and a proven track record over qualifications and accolades. Make sure you choose which is right for you.

Remember: all mentors can coach but not all coaches can mentor.

PROGRAMMES VS TAILORED

The next question to consider is whether you want to follow a structured programme which often repeats, or whether you want a more bespoke experience that focusses on what YOU want all the time rather than just some of the time.

With a structured programme, you should know what to expect as you go through the programme, and you will know how long it takes. This may be just what you are looking for, but it can mean you are directed towards a path you might not always want to follow, so check the programme covers exactly what you want and need.

Programmes typically start from 3 months. It's not often you find a programme that takes longer than a year, although you can of course repeat the programme.

Tailored sessions mean you get to decide what you want to work on, and for how long. This is more fl xible and totally geared towards your business. Think of it like a 'pick n mix' or 'all you can eat' buffet

REGULAR VS ON-DEMAND SESSIONS

If you have a specific challenge or area you want to work on, you might want to have just one or two on-demand sessions. Generally, the more regular your contact with your coach or mentor, the quicker your results will come. Most coaches will offer weekly, fortnightly or monthly sessions. Franchised coaches might not offer on-demand sessions, but most independent coaches will.

Whomever you are thinking about working with, the first step has to be an 'alignment' session, which should be a free, to check if there is a good fit between you both and whether they have a solution to match your requirements. This is a great way to find out what they are like, how they work and of course how much they charge (if you can't find it on their website). So make sure you always make use of this before you commit to working with a particular mentor or coach. **Please also be mindful of those who are quick to offer and promise a solution without fully understanding your aims and objectives.**

FIXED PRICE VS COMMISSION

Some coaches will work on a commission basis, where you pay a modest monthly retainer, and then on top of this you will pay a percentage of the additional profit you make after you start working with them. This needs to be very carefully considered and properly fixed in a contract, as you can imagine.

DO BUSINESS COACHES OFFER A GUARANTEE?

It is unusual for a business coach to offer a guarantee as results often depend on the actions you, the client, take. You can of course ask them for results previous clients have achieved and a good place to start would be their testimonials and recommendations which you can research independently.

You may also find it useful to look at their LinkedIn profile for posts, articles and especially comments on those articles as they can give you a real insight into what others think.

You will find the most common guarantee is 'money back or free coaching' from those with a proven track record and a body of work and/or experience to back it up. **Be mindful of those who are unwilling to commit to a guarantee since it is impossible to have one without enough research into what YOU want and need.** A strong opening question you can ask in your alignment session.

A WORD ON PRIORITIES

Whatever your position, role, age or size of your business, whether solo or as a leader in a growing team, your aims and objectives should always take precedent. Our job as coaches and mentors is to make what we do fit with what you want, not to make you fit or conform to a system - that's my belief.

The person or organisation you ultimately choose to work with must help you discover what you want and then take you on a journey that reveals your aims and objectives at a pace that solidifies your results

See also
Possibilities and Probabilities (p133)
What Does Making Changes In Business Really Mean? (p163)
How To Keep Your Battery Charged (p187)
What's The Difference Between A Teacher, A Mentor And A Coach? (p219)

What Can I Do Now To Prepare?

Just before the end of 'lock-down', following the Covid-19 pandemic, I had been polling people and asking them what was mostly on their mind and what was on the mind of their clients.

By far the biggest question was "What can I do now to prepare for when we re-start?"

Most people seemed to be thinking about new ways to make what they do more accessible to their clients and recognised that learning new ways to do things was a first step

The explosion in courses, webinars and training videos created an amazing resource for us all to share and use our knowledge, but I think it's really important to remember it's not what we learn but what we do with it.

There are three types of people in the world, those who make things happen, those who watch things happen and those who find reasons why things don't happen for them.

If you are going to invest in a workshop, a course or any amount of learning (even reading this book cover to cover) make sure you are prepared to take action, otherwise you're just wasting your time. The time you need is not just about absorbing the learning, it's implementing what you learn and getting long term support, so your actions and plans brings results forever.

Time To Dry Off ...

Mark Jarvis

About the Author

Mark Jarvis is a business mentor and coach, entrepreneur business owner of 30+ years, MD, NED, investor, author and speaker. He is a proud family man and a big fan of motorsport, architecture, coffee and ca e.

Mark is a specialist in helping people to grow and organisations to start-up, scale-up and sell-up. He works with owners, directors, partners and leaders by supporting them on their own growth journey which means that they get results faster through highly energised teams.

He has studied relational business growth for over 20 years, has a Masters degree in Business Intelligence, ILM 7 Diploma, and CIPD accreditations, and is a member of the Association of Business Mentors. He is widely recognised as an expert in professional networking, improving sales, growing people, teams and culture within organisations, inspiring businesses to scale profitably to exit, and is an international super-connector.

Mark began his business journey in the early 1990s and continues to start, build, buy, sell and invest in businesses across the UK having spent over 15 years in customer service training and management. With a proven track record across multiple industries, including design and marketing, information technology, property, franchising, legal and financial businesses, retail, hotels and hospitality amongst many others, he helps businesses to grow people, enhance processes, protect the planet, develop products and increase profitabilit .

Mark believes that every person, business and organisation has the potential to grow beyond their current limitations by surrounding themselves with the right people and investing in the right knowledge. His mission is to build a better, stronger, smarter and more sustainable future for small and medium enterprises by accelerating their growth and compounding their profitabilit .

Mark has an innovative way of thinking that brings change and inspires growth. His insights and wisdom in relational growth strategies bring better quality, consistency and security to all businesses and organisations that are committed to their future.

> "Growth is the ability to follow someone into something that's new in order to build something that's great."

MJ

Endorsements

Thank you to these wonderful people who took time out of their busy schedules to read and endorse my book. Here are their endorsements in full.

If you're looking for a business book that offers practical dvice without the flu , Mark Jarvis's *The Very Best Business Handbook You'll Ever Own (Unless You Use It as a Bookend)* is an excellent choice. Mark is an experienced professional and business mentor, and provides a straightforward approach to starting, scaling, and selling a business. His philosophy - People x Processes x Planet x Products x Profitability = Sustainable Success - is a proven formula that covers all aspects of business growth.

What sets Mark's book apart is its emphasis on practical, real-world solutions. Each chapter is designed to give you actionable insights that you can implement immediately. The book is organised with handy icons and a clear index, allowing you to find relevant topics quickl .

Whether you're an aspiring entrepreneur or an established business leader, this handbook is your guide to achieving sustainable success. Keep it on your desk for when you need a quick boost of inspiration or a simple solution to a business problem. It's not just a book - it's your new business partner.

Claire Boscq
No 1 Woman Customer Experience Global Gurus
Keynote Speaker and The BizShui Creator

Mark Jarvis's book is a masterclass in practical business wisdom, combining decades of real-world experience with actionable advice for entrepreneurs at all stages of their business journey. Mark is a seasoned business mentor and entrepreneur, leverages his extensive background in various industries to craft a guide that is both comprehensive and incredibly accessible.

The author's philosophy is straightforward yet profound: he believes in simplifying the complex world of business without reducing its challenges to mere trivialities. This approach is evident in every chapter of the book, where Mark distils complex business concepts into digestible, implementable strategies that resonate with both novice entrepreneurs and seasoned business leaders.

What sets this book apart is Mark and his commitment to practicality. He goes beyond mere theory, offering readers a treasure trove of real-life examples, personal anecdotes, and insightful reflections on his own successes and setbacks. This method not only makes the book relatable but also ensures that readers can see the practical application of each lesson in their day-to-day business operations.

Moreover, Mark's simple writing style is engaging and infused with a motivational tone that encourages readers to take action and pursue their business goals with renewed vigor. His passion for fostering sustainable success through people, processes, and profitability shines throughout the book, making it not just a read but a journey of learning and empowerment.

In conclusion, this is more than just a business book; it's a mentorship in paperback form, packed with invaluable lessons and insights that are bound to make a significant impact on any business venture.

Whether you're looking to start, scale, or sell a business, Mark Jarvis's book is an essential resource that promises to guide you towards achieving sustainable success in the often-turbulent world of business.

Jamie McAnsh
Inspirational Keynote Speaker & TEDx Presenter,
Head of Inclusion for Champions (UK) Plc

How many books do you read? I mean really read, understand, and from those take action and implement?

Over the years I have spoken to many business owners who are avid readers; strangely they all suggest the next best read. When I look at their business I am aware that the read may have been the best, but it has not changed their approach, delivery or indeed, their return from being really busy and chasing their tails. They still say, "We still need more of the right clients," or, "I wish I had more time."

You may never of heard of Mark Jarvis. May I take a moment to share with you why for the past 5 years I have a weekly discussion with him.

Mark is a professional of the highest order, always adding value to conversations and being a go to person. His ability to understand issues and concerns of those around him is impactful and his support of clients is second to none.

Outside of business he can be found most weekends in the season around racetracks where he has an overseeing marshalling role, a family man and proud grandad. A very kind and caring person.

Please now having selected this book read it on purpose, implement from its content and follow the process the chapters lead you through. There are some quick wins, some will take a little longer however providing it not used as a book end, you will with its content create the outcomes you desire.

Phillip Burton
Master Coach, Consultant and Trainer

I wish this book had been there when I started my business!

By far, this is the only book you need: Mark Jarvis', *The Very Best Business Handbook You'll Ever Own (Unless You Use It as a Bookend)* - it covers everything essential for achieving long-lasting success in both new and well-established businesses!

Mark has this truly remarkable and admirable ability to blend his extensive knowledge and expertise, accumulated over decades across various sectors, into a modern and comprehensive guide. His book captures the essence of timeless principles that have stood the test of time while seamlessly incorporating AI and contemporary strategies.

This unique and genius combination ensures your business will be more efficien and profitable, bridging the gap between traditional wisdom and modern innovation.

Olga Geidane
Author and keynote speaker on self-leadership and relationships. Mindset coach, event host and MC Professional Speaking Association President

Acknowledgements

There are too many! If I were to list all the people I've learned from and all the people that have helped and supported me, this page would be longer than the book. From my English and Music teachers at school, to the chef's and managers who mentored me in my early days in the hotel industry, right through to those who supported me in my early days in business, but most importantly, my family who stood by me when things got tough and celebrated with me when things were great.

Feels like one of those Oscar acceptance speeches but it does feel right to thank and acknowledge all those that have shared my journey, without them I wouldn't be where I am today, and I wouldn't be able to offer the experiences, insights and support I am now able to give.

Finally, a huge thank you to all my mentors and coaches past and present, you know who you are – thank you! And a final final thank you to all my fellow authors and speakers, only some I've been able to reference in this book, without you many of the ideas I've learned, developed and implemented in my own businesses would not have taken shape, again, thank you, it's an honour and pleasure to learn from you.

Mark

Mark Jarvis

References

Books

Bachelder, Cheryl, *Dare to Serve: How to Drive Superior Results by Serving Others*, (Berrett-Koehler), 2015
Collins, Jim & Jerry I. Porras, Built to Last: Successful Habits of Visionary Companies, (HarperCollins), 1994
Tabart, Benjamin, The History of Jack and the Bean-Stalk, (Unknown), 1734
Sinek, Simon, The Infinite Game, (enguin Random House), 2019
Vaynerchuk, Gary, The Thank You Economy, (HarperCollins), 2011
Rohn, Jim & Widener Chris, Jim Rohn's 8 Best Success Lessons, (Blackstone Publishing), 2014
Adams, Douglas, The Hitchhikers Guide To The Galaxy, (Pan Books), 1979
Dahl, Roald, Charlie and the Chocolate Factory, (Alfred A. Knopf, Inc.), 1964

Websites

Barnes, Melody & Schmitz, Paul, *Community Engagement Matters (Now More Than Ever)* Stanford Social Innovation Review, https://ssir.org 01/10/23
Chen, Alex, *Triple Filter Test*, (Weekly Wisdom Blog), https://www.weeklywisdomblog.com/post/socrates-triple-filte -test 28/06/2024
Davenport, Thomas H. & Mittal, Nitin, *Generative AI: What Is It, Tools, Models, Applications and Use Cases*, https://hbr.org 01/03/24
Dunbar, R.I.M., (2010), *Coevolution of neocortical size, group size and language in humans*, Cambridge University Press, https://www.cambridge.org/core/journals/behavioral-and-brain-sciences/article/abs/coevolution-of-neocortical-size-group-size-and-language-in-humans/4290FF4D7362511136B9A15A96E74FEF 30/04/19
Editorial Team, *6 in 10 of start-up businesses do fail in their first 5 years*, British Business Bank, https://www.british-business-bank.co.uk 30/06/22
Editorial Team, Getting Predictable Referrals, Assentiv, https://asentiv.com 30/06/19

Editorial Team, *Homepage*, ActionCoach, https://actioncoach.co.uk 28/06/24

Editorial Team, *Homepage*, Bing, https://www.bing.com 28/06/24

Editorial Team, *Homepage*, Business Doctors, https://businessdoctors.co.uk 28/06/24

Editorial Team, *Homepage*, ChatGPT, https://chatbotapp.ai 28/06/24

Editorial Team, *Homepage*, The Entrepreneurs Circle https://entrepreneurscircle.org May-24

Editorial Team, *Homepage*, Entrepreneurs Operating System, https://www.eosworldwide.com 28/06/24

Editorial Team, *Homepage*, Google, www.google.co.uk 28/06/24

Editorial Team, How to stop the Great Resignation, Everything DiSC, (John Wiley & Sons, Inc), https://www.everythingdisc.com/blogs/management-blog/ 28/06/24

Editorial Team, *Homepage*, Instagram, https://www.instagram.com 28/06/24

Editorial Team, *Homepage*, LinkedIn, https://www.linkedin.com 28/06/24

Editorial Team, *Homepage*, Microsoft, https://www.microsoft.com/en-gb 28/06/24

Editorial Team, *Homepage*, Viant, https://www.viantinc.com 28/06/24

Editorial Team, *Homepage*, Zoom, https://zoom.us 28/06/24

Editorial Team, *iPhone*, Apple, https://www.apple.com/iphone/ 28/06/24

Editorial Team, *State of the Global Workplace*, https://www.gallup.com/workplace/349484/state-of-the-global-workplace.aspx 28/06/24

Reichheld, Frederick, *The One Number You Need to Grow*, https://hbr.org/2003/12/the-one-number-you-need-to-grow 31/12/23

Ribeiro, Lucio, *Decoding 2024: Experts unravel AI's next big phase*, https://www.forbes.com.au/news/innovation/decoding-2024-experts-unravel-ais-next-big-phase/ 28/06/24

Wikipedia Contributors, *Charles Blondin*, (Wikipedia, The Free Encyclopaedia), https://en.wikipedia.org/wiki/Charles_Blondin 28/06/2024

Wikipedia Contributors, *CVS Pharmacies*, (Wikipedia, The Free Encyclopaedia), https://en.wikipedia.org/wiki/CVS_Pharmacy 28/06/24

Wikipedia Contributors, *DISC assessment*, (Wikipedia, The Free Encyclopaedia), https://en.wikipedia.org/wiki/DISC_assessment 28/06/24

Wikipedia Contributors, *Earnings before interest, taxes, depreciation and amortization (EBITDA)*, (Wikipedia, The Free Encyclopaedia), https://en.wikipedia.org/wiki/Earnings_before_interest,_taxes,_depreciation_and_amortization 28/06/24

Wikipedia Contributors, *Kaizen*, (Wikipedia, The Free Encyclopaedia), https://en.wikipedia.org/wiki/Kaizen 31/01/20

Wikipedia Contributors, *Key performance indicators (KPI's)*, (Wikipedia, The Free Encyclopaedia), https://en.wikipedia.org/wiki/Performance_indicator 28/06/24

Wikipedia Contributors, *Larry Merlo*, (Wikipedia, The Free Encyclopaedia), https://en.wikipedia.org/wiki/Larry_Merlo 28/06/24

Wikipedia Contributors, *Net Promotor Score*, (Wikipedia, The Free Encyclopaedia), https://en.wikipedia.org/wiki/Net_promoter_score 28/06/24

Wikipedia Contributors, *Second Law of Thermodynamics*, (Wikipedia, The Free Encyclopaedia), https://en.wikipedia.org/wiki/Second_law_of_thermodynamics 28/06/24

Wikipedia Contributors, *Socrates*, (Wikipedia, The Free Encyclopaedia), https://en.wikipedia.org/wiki/Socrates 28/06/24

Wikipedia Contributors, *SWOT Analysis*, (Wikipedia, The Free Encyclopaedia), https://en.wikipedia.org/wiki/SWOT_analysis 28/06/24

Film

Cameron, James, *The Terminator*, (Orion Pictures), 1984

Herek, Stephen, *Bill & Ted's Excellent Adventure*, (Orion Pictures), 1989

Ramis, Harold, *Groundhog Day*, (Columbia Pictures), 1993

De Palma, Brian, *Mission Impossible*, (Cruise/Wagner Productions), 1996

Johnston, Joe, *Captain America: The First Avenger*, (Marvel Studios), 2011

Mark Jarvis

Index

Symbols

5% Solution 169

A

Academy for Scaling Businesses 153, 154
Accountability 153, 154
ActionCoach 238
Adey, Abbirose iv
Artificial Intelligence (AI) 32, 33, 35, 36, 37, 38, 39, 40, 41, 42, 43
Asana 231

B

Bachelder, Cheryl 18
Bain and Co. 183
Bain & Company 44
  Reichheld, Frederick 44
Bill and Ted 109
Blame 64, 234
Blondin, Charles 131, 132
Business Doctors 238

C

Captain America 223, 224
Change 163, 164, 165
ChatGPT4 42
Collins, Jim 46
Compensation 30, 33, 77
Covid-19 111, 242
Cox, Brian 125
Creative Distraction 65, 68, 69
Credibility 149, 150, 157
Cultural Success 71
CVS Pharmacies 14

D

Delegation , 45, 46, 47, 48, 49, 50, 51, 52, 54, 87, 90, 91, 9
DISC 100
Dunbar, Robin 143

E

Energy Levels 187
Entrepreneurs Operating System 238

F

Focus 85, 86, 87, 88, 89, 90, 91, 129, 173
Forbes 36

G

GALLUP 78
Google 4, 37, 42, 201
Groundhog Day 117

H

Harvard Business Review 40
Hewlett Packard 223

Hitchhikers Guide To The Galaxy 209
Hubspot 231

I
Influencers 4
Instagram 40

J
Jobs, Steve 224

K
Kaizen 200
KPI 62

L
Leadership Development Strategy 45, 47, 53, 99
LinkedIn 29, 32, 62, 241

M
MacDowell, Andie 118
Marketing Strategy 19, 61, 96, 135, 151, 155, 205, 207
Mentor 26, 27, 41, 42, 118, 189, 218, 219, 220, 221, 175, 237, 239, 240
Merlo, Larry 14
Microsoft 42
 Bing 42, 43
Mission Impossible 215
Mission Obsessed 20
Momentum 102, 129
Monday.com 231
Murray, Bill 117

N
Net Promotor Score 4
Niagara 131, 132
Not-For-Profit Organisations , 11, 14, 18, 23, 77, 83, 9

O
Organisational Culture 20, 26, 33, 46, 47, 52, 232

P
Packard, David 223
Perpetual Motion Business 215, 216
Plateau 71, 73, 74
Priorities Conflict 6
Probation Period 22
Problem Market Fit 58, 60
Product Market Fit 57, 58, 60
Profitability 149, 150, 15
Psychometric Profiling 31, 3
 DISC 101, 113
Purpose 11, 12, 13, 14, 15, 16, 17, 18, 19, 20, 21, 22, 61, 72, 77, 78, 79, 80, 23, 81, 82, 83

R
Recruitment 19, 20, 21, 22, 23, 25, 26, 27, 28, 30, 32, 33, 62
References 22
Referral Partners 123
Referrals 44, 62, 122, 123, 135, 137, 138, 139, 140, 141, 151, 155, 167, 168, 169, 172, 179, 183, 204, 195, 203, 204, , 205, 206, 114
Relationship Pipeline 9, 167, 168
Rohn, Jim 159
ROI 206

S
Sales Pipeline 9, 28, 167, 168
Scheduling Conflict 6
Sinek, Simon 168
Slack 39

Social Responsibility 19, 20, 57
Socrates 109
Stanford Social Innovation
	Review 17
Start-up Businesses 57, 58, 59, 60, 71
Sustainable Success 42, 84
SWOT Analysis 85

T

Teamwork 231
Terminator 36, 39
The Entrepreneurs Circle 238
Time Limited Turnover 73, 225, 226
Triple Filter Test 109, 110

V

Vaynerchuk, Gary 177
Visibility 149, 150
Vision 1, 2, 3, 4, 5, 6, 7, 8, 12, 19, 20, 21, 61, 66, 67, 82, 95, 102, 148, 190, 232
Vision Inventory 7, 8

W

Wikipedia 125, 201
Winning Culture 72, 74
Word-of-Mouth 5, 6, 80

Z

Zoom 181, 182

Mark Jarvis

Your Notes

Please use the following pages to make any notes, observations or questions you may have about the themes in this book. I would love to have a conversation with you about your ideas and thoughts. Please contact me via mark-jarvis.co.uk

Mark Jarvis

Mark Jarvis

Mark Jarvis

Mark Jarvis

www.ingramcontent.com/pod-product-compliance
Lightning Source LLC
Chambersburg PA
CBHW061214070526
44584CB00029B/3835